Our Children

Our Responsibility

Our Children
Our Responsibility

Keeping Our Kids S.A.F.E., Preschool to High School

by

Timothy C. Derby

Project Our Children Our Responsibility

2311 Hwy. 45 North, Suite D

Columbus, MS 39705

U.S.A.

www.safecarechildren.com

Library of Congress Cataloging—in—Publication Data

Derby, Timothy C.

Our Children Our Responsibility: keeping our kids safe from preschool to high school—1st ed.

1. Child Safety   2. Safety

Library of Congress Control Number: 2003112600

ISBN: 0-9729465-2-7

First Published in 2003 by:

Nicole-Ashley Publishing

MISSION STATEMENT

Children are not only our most valuable resources for the future, but they are also precious gifts. God has not only blessed us with children, but has literally entrusted them to us. It is our responsibility, as adults, to protect those who are unable to protect themselves. My goal for the **S.A.F.E.** program is to assist adults in fulfilling that roll so that our kids can do what they do best — enjoy being kids.

****

Acknowledgments

I have devoted most of my life to training and instructing others in the traditional art of karate. While my goal has always been to influence those that I teach in a positive way, I never imagined taking on the roll of child safety advocate. However, I firmly believe that it is our responsibility to go in the direction that the Lord leads us. As this great challenge continues to unfold, I am thankful for the ability, as well as the opportunities, I have been given and continue to receive. I also humbly acknowledge that it is God who works in me both to will and to do His good pleasure, and to Him go all the praise, honor and glory.

I would also like to acknowledge someone who, while most often is working behind the scenes, never receives the recognition she truly deserves - my precious wife, Kathy. Her abilities, as well as her commitment to excellence, never ceases to amaze me.

To Ashley and Hunter

CONTENTS

Chapter Three : Child Abduction

Chapter Four : Internet The Information Highway

Chapter Five : School Bullying

INTRODUCTION

Recently, through vast media coverage, we have seen what appears to be an unbelievable outbreak of child victimization. Whether it is child abductions, sexual abuse, or school violence, the problems appear to be reaching almost epic proportions. We are just beginning to understand how serious an issue we are facing. What can we do to assure the safety of our children? Rather than just concentrate on what we can do, we often find answers by searching out what we can't do. To begin with, gone are the days when we could allow our children to roam unsupervised in the neighborhoods, parks, or shopping centers. While most people are "good," there are countless numbers of those who seek to harm our children. Also, gone are the days where we can look at the threats made by children at school as simply idle threats. We have seen first hand just how serious these situations can be. Does this all mean that we should avoid contact with others in society by locking up our children? The obvious answer is no; however, it is dangerous to think that we can simply ignore these problems and hope they will go away.

First and foremost, when discussing child victimization, we must overcome the attitude that "It can never happen to my child." Without acceptance, there is little chance for avoidance. However, it is equally dangerous to assume the attitude that "It will happen to my child."

Though we should be deeply concerned with the safety of our children, we must not, through our own paranoia, force our fears on them. Keep in mind however, that fear itself is not necessarily bad. When one loses all fear toward certain subjects or situations, carelessness usually follows. What is important is that we, as well as our children, learn to control fear, rather than allow it to control us. The most effective and efficient way to control fear is through education.

Our Children Our Responsibility, which is based on the **(S.A.F.E.) Safety And Fear Education Program for Children**, serves as a comprehensive approach designed to instruct parents, educators, and children in specific areas of personal child safety. This book is divided into seven chapters. Chapter one is designed to explain how adults and children can work collectively in their efforts to assist in developing the most effective program for personal child safety. Chapters two through five consists of specific safety issues. Following the introductions, each "safety chapter" begins with a description of the predators who attempt to harm children, as well as how and why they operate. The chapters continue by separating fact from fiction, therefore shedding some insight into each safety issue by discussing some of the major misconceptions surrounding child safety. The safety chapters conclude with specific prevention tips, that can and should be applied to promote the prevention of victimization against children. Chapter six offers essential steps that can be taken in the event your child is victimized. Chapter seven concludes this book by offering insight into methods for effectively teaching safety principles to your own child.

The task of protecting children from victimization is a difficult one. Being a karate practitioner for nearly 20 years, I have learned that in order to accomplish any difficult task, one must first formulate a plan. The book you now hold in your hand offers you that plan. **You will find this book is much more than merely an overview of today's problems facing child safety. It will serve as a proactive approach toward the prevention of victimization against our children.** What could be more important than protecting our children? Though they only make up 25 percent of our population, children are 100 percent of our future.

Note to Parents

Being an educator, as well as a father of two, I understand the difficulties faced when attempting to speak to children about various forms of victimization. My advice is that you deal with your child openly and honestly. However, make no mistake about it, I firmly believe that we should not only protect our children physically, but also emotionally. It is neither necessary nor appropriate to be too explicit with a child, especially those that are younger. **It is possible to teach children tactfully, without forcing them to face many of the adult issues and fears that we understand.** Our society already forces our children to grow up much too quickly. The most important thing we can offer our children is a loving and nurturing home; one that offers them the sense of security they deserve. Children should be taught methods for self-protection, but even more important, children must "feel" safe and be allowed to do what they do best, and that is to enjoy being a child.

I encourage you, as you read and study this book, to look for ways of implementing it. Knowledge must be applied in order to be useful. Also, I encourage you to review, not only particular points of interest, but this books entire contents and reinforce the principles with your child regularly. Studies have proven time and again that so called "single hit" instruction is not a very effective form of learning. **We also should not approach any child safety program as a chore, but rather look at it as a safe and educated lifestyle.** I have found that most often an "educated" child leads to a "confident" child and a "confident" child leads to a "safe" child.

God Bless You and God Bless Our Children,

Tim Derby

About the Author

Tim Derby has devoted nearly two decades to studying traditional karate. He has committed the past 14 years to training adults and children from all backgrounds and has served as an advisor to countless law enforcement and educational agencies in specific areas of personal child safety and development. As the founder of American te-jitsu Karate, he has earned black belts in four individual styles, of which three he has achieved a Master's degree. As a karate and child safety advocate, as well as father of two, Tim is the founder of the **(S.A.F.E.) Safety And Fear Education and (C.A.R.E.) Character And Respect Education Programs for Children.** These programs are designed to instruct parents, educators, and children in specific areas of personal child safety and character development. As a result of these programs, Tim received a personal White House invitation from President George W. Bush to represent his state and attend the first ever White House Conference on child safety convened by the President himself. Currently, through the nonprofit organization, "Project Our Children Our Responsibility" founded by Tim and his wife, Kathy, he is reaching thousands of children each year as he coordinates with various government and educational agencies and organizations to implement the S.A.F.E. and C.A.R.E. programs in schools throughout the state of Mississippi, as well as other states. Also, to Tim Derby's credit are two additional books entitled: *Using Your Fear, A Four Step Guide to Women's Self - Defense and Black Belt Karate for Children, Added Ability Added Responsibility.* In addition to being a full time speaker and author, Tim owns and instructs the BodyFit Karate and Fitness Center in Columbus, MS, which he established in 1989.

The Predator

I t still surprises me to see the expression on parents faces when discovering that there are some sick people in our society who seek out and attempt to harm our children. It is vital that parents, not only accept that there are such individuals, but also understand something about them. There is a saying used in karate that states, **"If you do not know your enemy you will very likely fall prey to that enemy."** In other words, how can we avoid placing our children at risk if we do not know anything about the ones from whom we are protecting them? While it is enough to explain to children that there are "bad people" who do 'bad things," parents need to know much more. To be effective in protecting our children, we must understand who these disturbed people are, why they do what they do, as well as how they operate. Though this area of study can and should be quite disturbing, the benefits of learning how these individuals work can have a profound effect on our methods for protecting children.

As we go through the various sections of this book, we will go into more detail about specific types of people who target children. What is important to know right now is that all of these so called bad people share one thing in common. **They are all "predators."** There are basically two levels of predatory behavior. The level one predators go about their everyday activities much like you and me. These people are called opportunists. While these particular predators may not go through each day looking for a specific victim, if an opportunity presents itself, they are ready to capitalize on it. The second level (the most dangerous) is the predator in the purest sense. These individuals, rather than wait for a situation to present itself, go through their day looking to create their own opportunity. This type of predator is very effective. This person, because this is his lifestyle, knows all the tricks of the trade. **He can be intimidating, tricky, seductive and even charming at times.** These predators have learned, through experience, exactly what is necessary to carry out their twisted purposes.

If there is any good news about the predator, it is that in order for him to take action, there must be an opportunity. Through effective education, as well as responsible parenting, it is very possible to prevent those opportunities, thus putting a stop to predatory behavior before it begins.

Chapter One

Sharing
the Responsibility

1

CHAPTER ONE

Sharing the Responsibility

The Foundation of the S.A.F.E. program is rooted in its coordinated effort between parents, teachers (educators) and the children themselves. Any program that lacks this comprehensive approach is destined to fall short in its ability to protect our children. Though it is a joint effort, there is an order to the responsibility for all those involved. This first chapter divides that responsibility between parents, teachers, and children, as well as provides insight to assist all those involved in better fulfilling their particular roll concerning personal child safety.

> - **Children's Responsibility**
> - **School's Responsibility**
> - **Parent's Responsibility**

CHILDREN'S RESPONSIBILITY

I am firmly committed to the principle that all children must learn how to protect themselves. After all, children do represent the **"last line"** of defense. I also believe that children should share the least amount of responsibility. **It is not very realistic to believe that a child can match wits with an adult.** Consider for a moment, how many times you have been persuaded or literally pressured into doing things. For example, how often have you gone into a department store to purchase one item, only to have a skilled salesperson somehow convince you to purchase twice as much as you intended? This analogy may seem irrelevant, but imagine just how effectively some adults persuade or even trick other adults. Now multiply that effect ten fold and that's the ability an adult has in persuading a child. Does this mean that it is useless to devote time to teaching children how to protect themselves? Of course the answer is no; it is vital that children know how to apply protection principles. **The point is, that if we rely on children to play the primary role in their overall protection, we are destined to fail.**

SCHOOL'S RESPONSIBILITY

Schools serve a major roll in not only the academic excellence of a student, but also a student's overall personal safety. When you consider that many children spend more waking hours at school than they do in their own homes, it becomes clear that schools have a tremendous responsibility concerning the type of environment they provide for students.

- Administrators -

School administrators must work diligently to create a safe learning environment for all students. First and foremost, efforts must be made to assure that a school provides a physically secure environment whereby school perimeters, as well as children, are monitored and adequately supervised before, during, and after school. Secondly, it is the responsibility of school administration to provide students with a safe school "climate." In other words, school administration must communicate with the students and assure them that their personal safety is of the utmost importance, so that each individual student "feels" safe.

- Teachers -

Aside from immediate family, few people have as much influence over a child as a teacher. Consequently, teachers have a special opportunity to contribute to the personal safety of their students. Obviously teachers can assist in reinforcing school safety policies by supervising children, as well as offer specific safety tips, etc.... Additionally, teachers can assist in a student's personal development, which in turn, affects that student's safety. One principle that is mentioned throughout this book is the fact that a confident child most often leads to a safe child. Regardless of the type of victimization, children who lack confidence and self-esteem are vulnerable to such an extreme that they often represent an easy target. Through encouragement and various forms of positive reinforcement, a teacher can help a student become more self-confident and aware of his/her self-worth.

Following is a recent experience I had with a teacher who taught children in the five to eight-year-old range. I witnessed this teacher instructing on a number of occasions, and while quite demanding (which I applaud), she was also verbally abusive with the students (which I do not approve of). This teacher said many negative statements to the children and showed no sign of positive reinforcement. I had an opportunity to speak to her after one of her classes, and she asked me how I thought she was doing. While it was not my intent to criticize her, I did feel an obligation to explain to her what I believe is the responsibility of a teacher. I explained that in her life time she will likely teach more than a thousand students, at best she will remember only a select few. However, each of her impressionable aged students will most likely have memories of her for the rest of their lives. I informed her that as educators, it is our responsibility to work diligently with our children so that those memories are positive reflections. I then asked her if she had any particular teacher that influenced her life. She immediately said the name of a teacher who had a tremendous influence over her. She went on to state that it was because of this teacher's encouragement that she herself pursued her degree in the field of education. I informed her that she too could be such a teacher and that the choice was entirely hers. Through our continued discussion, we spoke about how easy it is for teachers to fall into a rut with the attitude that all they are paid for is to teach their particular subject. This approach to teaching is a huge disservice to our children. Any educator, who is not concerned with the overall welfare and development of children, should seriously consider another profession.

The bottom line is that whether teachers choose to or not, they will influence each student they teach in some form or fashion. This influence can be positive or negative. The influence may be meaningless or it could be life changing. The teacher, who is willing to take that extra step and offer encouragement to a student, is then contributing tremendously to that student's personal safety.

PARENT'S RESPONSIBILITY

Regardless of what society implies, parents still have the greatest influence over the lives of their children. For this reason, parents must assume the responsibility for their child's safety. WE CAN NEVER ASSURE THAT OUR CHILDREN

ARE 100 PERCENT SAFE, BUT THERE ARE MANY MEASURES WE CAN TAKE THAT WILL ASSIST THEM IN BEING SAFER! The following are four distinct areas in which parents can assume responsibility for the safety of their children.

-Instruction-

School and community safety programs are very beneficial; however, **nothing compares to the instruction of a parent**. No one knows your child better than you; no one knows his/her fears or concerns, likes, and dislikes. So, who could possibly be more suited to instruct children when dealing with such personal issues? It should be obvious that the parents should play the most important role in a child's safety. For the most, their child is their primary concern. However, **simply being concerned about child safety is not enough**. In order to be effective, parents must do two important things. First and foremost, you must be equipped. It is virtually impossible to teach a child anything unless you are thoroughly educated in that particular subject yourself. You must first devote adequate time to educating yourself. Secondly, you must take an active approach in teaching your child. In doing so, you can look for opportunities to teach your child when he/she may be the most receptive. For example, a child may see a T.V. show or even a news story, where a child is abducted or sexually abused, etc., and asks you what would you do if something happened to him/her. It is during such times that children are very receptive to what you may teach them. As parents, we should look for such windows of opportunity to introduce specific safety issues. Children are much brighter than we often think. They are extremely capable of absorbing and understanding information. **Our job as parents is to speak to them openly and honestly and to instruct them often.**

-Encouragement-

Even at a very young age, today's society has a tendency to place our children in a very competitive arena. **While it is important to motivate children, quite often we, as parents, add to the problem by being much too critical.** If I have learned anything through my experiences as an instructor, I have learned that nothing builds confidence in a child more than positive reinforcement. I am not implying that one should never reprimand their child. To allow a child to go through life without any form of correction or even discouragement at times would be a total disservice to the overall development of that child. However, as a parent, **you should look for every opportunity to encourage your child.** It is important to acknowledge a child's accomplishments and equally important are his/her genuine efforts. Most parents will agree that it is important to provide both financially and materially for our children. What is even more important is that we provide for our children emotionally. **By devoting our time to our children, and at the same time encouraging them, we help them feel both loved and secure.** It is that secure child who is usually the more confident child, and one who will understand the principle of self-worth. We should always keep in mind that, in addition to teaching our children how to be safe, we must also make sure they "feel safe." There is no better foundation for emotional security than the love and encouragement of a parent.

-Lifestyle-

Much has been said about the lifestyles of particular families whose children have been victimized, but it is important that we realize no family is completely immune to these issues. It is also important to emphasize that regardless of the lifestyle, no family deserves to have their child fall victim to a violent crime. **I have studied many cases where a family's lifestyle did not necessarily invite situations, but at the same time, did not do anything to prevent them.** It is definitely not my intention to indict parents, but I do believe that parents must realize the necessity of living a sacrificial lifestyle. Though thankfully not the majority, many parents treat their children as a total imposition and often carry on the same lifestyle they had before becoming parents. These parents go wherever they want, and have little regard for the welfare of their child, often leaving them with questionable people or even at home alone. These parents live the type of self-indulged lifestyle that not only demonstrates neglect, but also can eventually lead to a child being at risk. **It is very important that all parents understand that they must be accountable for their actions**.

Equally as dangerous as neglect is ambivalence. **Parents quite often make decisions regardless of what one's better judgment tells them**. For example, a parent knows that leaving a child unattended in an automobile is dangerous. Rather than take the time and effort to get the child out, the parent thinks that since I am parked at the door and just running in and out, nothing could possibly happen. In making such a decision, you are not necessarily neglecting your child, and while most often nothing ever does happen, there are some cases where other parents have done the same thing and something tragic did happen. You do not need to look much farther than parks or even shopping malls to witness ambivalence. Based on the information provided by the media alone, most parents are coming to the realization that, whether in a public place or not, children cannot be left unattended. However, many parents still choose to ignore such logic and think that the odds are against something happening to their child. Parents are forced to make so many decisions concerning their children. **What is important is that you always take time to consider how those decisions could affect the safety of your children**.

-Supervision-

We live in a society where virtually everything our children do must be monitored. Surprisingly many parents fail to realize this fact or simply choose to ignore it. **The safety tips we teach our children are very beneficial, but they cannot and should not replace adult supervision.** Just as parents must take an active approach to educating their children, they must also exercise active supervision. To begin with, active supervision not only monitors the child, but also their perimeter. By actively monitoring the surrounding area, a parent is able to spot "potential" dangers or threats and respond accordingly. Secondly, active supervision monitors distance. For example, if your child is thirty feet away and some stranger approaches from the other direction and ends up only twenty feet away, that child is now at risk. Regardless of your supervision, the child is in harms way, because the stranger would have no problem closing that distance before you could protect them. This may sound extreme, but there have been cases where a stranger has driven right up to a playground and taken a child in direct view of his/her parents.

Finally, **effective active supervision must be undistracted**. The moment you are distracted, whether by a cell phone, laptop, or even other parents, your child is temporarily on his/her own. **The bottom line is that simply being present does not define effective supervision. Supervision must be active; it is the most effective measure one can take to help prevent a child from being at risk.**

CHAPTER ONE

Sharing the Responsibility Checklist

CHILD'S RESPONSIBILITY

- [ ] Understand the importance of child safety
- [ ] Study the basics of child safety yourself
- [ ] Obey the rules, they are designed for your overall safety
- [ ] Enjoy being a kid

TEACHER'S/EDUCATOR'S RESPONSIBILITY

- [ ] Be concerned with the safety and overall development of children you influence
- [ ] Make a positive impact on a child's life

SCHOOL'S RESPONSIBILITY

- [ ] Offer students a safe "environment"
- [ ] Provide student's with a safe "climate"

PARENT'S RESPONSIBILITY

- [ ] Instruct your children
- [ ] Exercise Active Supervision
- [ ] Encourage Your Child by telling them they are loved and show them by devoting your time to them
- [ ] Live a Sacrificial Lifestyle and lead by example

Chapter Two

Sexual Abuse
Against Children

2

CHAPTER TWO

Sexual Abuse

The United States Department of Justice estimates that there are approximately 300,000 reported cases of sexual abuse against children each year. What is so disturbing is that those reported incidents make up only a fraction of actual occurrences. Though intimidation and fear of family embarrassment contribute to many unreported cases, **the most common reason behind unreported sexual abuse is simply that no one other than the victim and the abuser usually knows.** This is why sexual abuse is so commonly referred to as the "secret" or "quiet" crime. The fact that sexual abuse is kept so secret, causes it to be a very difficult subject to understand.

Contributing to the difficulty of recognizing sexual abuse is the fact that, for the most part, the victim is seldom physically harmed. However, the psychological implications can be great. When children are victimized, they most often feel as though they have lost all sense of control; they also develop an overwhelming distrust toward others. Considering these negative effects of sexual abuse, it is vital that we do all we can to protect our children, as well as educate them regarding methods for protecting themselves, against this very serious area of abuse.

This chapter begins by defining sexual abuse. The chapter then goes into detail concerning who predators are, as well as how and why they target children. Also, we will uncover some of the basic misconceptions surrounding sexual abuse so we can be better prepared to tackle this disturbing issue. This chapter concludes with principles that are designed not only to further educate you in this specific area of child safety, but to also provide tried and true methods for prevention.

DEFINING SEXUAL ABUSE

Sexual abuse includes, but it not limited to, any form of improper touching (whether touching the child or asking the child to do so), child pornography, indecent exposure, or any form of an actual or implied sexual act. Basically, **child sexual abuse includes attempting ANYTHING with a child for the purpose of sexual gratification**.

THE ENEMY

As disturbing and surprising as it may be, there are some adults in our society who specifically prey on young children for sexual exploitations. Such acts are commonly referred to as pedophilia, and those involved in such behavior are known as pedophiles.

The pedophile is defined as one whose sexual preference is directed toward children. They can be women, but are almost always men. They may have a gender preference, but often their affections are directed toward both boys and girls. The United States Department of Justice states that the pedophile is known by the child nearly 90 percent of the time (i.e., acquaintances, family friends, immediate and extended family). Many think of a pedophile as the stereotypical perverted old man; however, this is seldom the case. **The frightening truth about a pedophile is that he can be absolutely anyone.** There is no effective profile for pedophiles. Their desire to stay anonymous motivates them to act and look as normal as you and me. They can be single or married, professionals or laborers, reputable people and even ministers. The list goes on and on. They may appear normal and harmless, but they are far from it.

MOTIVATION

(Why they do what they do)

As the characteristics of the pedophile vary, so too do their motivations. Many times the pedophile was abused himself. As a child, an abuser controlled him and he is merely carrying on the cycle of controlling others. **Most often the pedophile targets children to seek their nonjudgmental acceptance and affection**. What is most disturbing is that, unlike the basic child molester who may gain satisfaction by perversions such as exposing or fondling, the pedophile is often seeking an intimate relationship with the child. Equally disturbing is that usually pedophiles see nothing improper in their actions toward children. The Federal Bureau of Investigations reports that many pedophiles even believe that the children actually initiate the relationship by inviting sexual advances from the adult.

METHODS

(How They Operate)

Just as hunters have various methods they use when pursuing particular game, so does the predator have specific techniques in which he uses to entrap children. The following methods are, by no means all inclusive, but they do represent some of the most common ways the pedophile operates.

- Friendship-

While the family member may already have a child's trust, the non family member must first build trust between himself and the child. **This is accomplished by developing a friendship with the child, as well as the parents.** The pedophile will go to great lengths to build this trusting relationship. This time period can last a few days, weeks, or even months. It is not uncommon for this trust building period to last years before the pedophile initiates his actions toward the child.

-Keeping Secrets-

One of the primary strategies for the pedophile is secrecy. After developing a basic trust with the child, his first goal is to see how well the child keeps a secret. This may start with nothing more that an innocent game of telling a child something and implying that it is "our little secret." After testing the child and even teaching him/her to keep secrets, the pedophile quickly places the odds in his own favor.

-Attention/Affection-

Pedophiles capitalize on the fact that children need and even crave attention and affection. **They often prey on a child's innocence by persuading him/her, in their own subtle and seductive way that their perverted actions are actually natural and loving.** To the child, sadly enough, this often goes on for years before he/she understands that what is happening is improper.

-Curiosity-

Related to a child's innocence is his/her sense of curiosity. The pedophile understands this principle all too well. While children's curiosity is natural and can be healthy in their own development, the pedophile uses this to his own advantage. **He will often use children's curiosity of their own body, as well as others, as an open door for their exploitations**.

-Game Playing-

It is important to understand that not everyone who teases or wrestles around with a child is attempting to sexually abuse that child. However, these are very common methods used by the pedophile in order to initiate physical contact. One game often used by the pedophile is to hide an object, such as a coin, somewhere on the child's body (or his own) and then retrieve it, or allow the child to do so. As this progresses, the hiding places quickly end up in very discrete and private areas. He may also wrestle with the child to see how much physical contact he can pursue. **The pedophile uses such methods, often referred to as "grooming" in order to slowly train the child to remove all boundaries of physical touch**.

-Gift Givers-

Just as not every person who wrestles with children is attempting to abuse them, neither is a person who buys children various things necessarily attempting to bribe them. However, the pedophile has learned that bribery proves to be effective. He may purchase a child, something as elaborate as a pony, a bicycle, or something as simple as a piece of candy. This may not seem possible to you as an adult, but keep in mind we are talking about the mind of a child. **Basically, the pedophile is attempting to create leverage over the child, not necessarily implying that "if you do this for me I will do this for you," but rather in an attempt to receive a deep sense of emotional obligation from the child.**

WHY SEXUAL ABUSE CONTINUES

It is possible that sexual abuse can occur once to a child. However, this is most often the case only when a child is abused by a stranger, which is less than 10 percent of the time. **Approximately 90 percent of the time the abuser is known by the child and therefore has regular access to that child. For this reason, sexual abuse is most often a continual occurrence, at least until something or someone intervenes.** The question most often is, "Why do these incidents continue to occur?" The answer contains a great number of variables and could undoubtedly be a complete book in itself. Though the following, much like the motivations and techniques previously given are not all inclusive, they will shed some light on this question.

-Family Secrecy-

Sexual abuse against children is such a prevalent crime in our society primarily due to its secrecy. **When such issues arise inside a family, they are most often denied or even ignored**. While this is in part due to a desire to avoid possible criminal prosecution, as well as public ridicule, most adults in these families keep such an event secret simply to avoid the separation or breakup of the family. While this may sound noble, it is usually not necessarily because they understand the importance of family, but rather they don't want anything to disrupt their own lives, even at the expense of possibly ruining the life of the child involved.

-Victim Secrecy-

Once the pedophile has a child's complete trust, he will abuse him/her. It is then that the pedophile works diligently to assure that the child remains quiet, regarding his actions. He will usually begin by convincing the child that what they have is a special relationship. He will work to convince the child that no one else would understand, so it is very important that no one else knows. Soon afterward, the control sets in. The pedophile then convinces the child that what he/she has "allowed" to happen is bad. He attempts to place the blame on the child, therefore creating a sense of shame. **The child soon believes that he/she is to blame and will be punished if others find out.** The situation can also escalate to threats of physical violence. The pedophile usually threatens to harm the child, as well as those the child loves, if he/she were to ever tell anyone. For these reasons, as well as others, it is very common for children to carry the emotional scars of sexual abuse through their entire life, never revealing to anyone that they were victims.

-Need for Attention/Affection-

The most disturbing and what I believe to be the most disheartening reason for the continuance of individual sexual child abuse is how the pedophile capitalizes on a child's innocent desire for adult attention and affection. In these situations, the pedophile convinces the child that what he is doing is natural and caring, and that this is the way an adult shows children that he truly cares for them. **Sad as it may sound, there are children who are being victimized and are simply not aware that what is happening to them is wrong**.

MISCONCEPTIONS FACING

SEXUAL ABUSE

It appears as though people will go to great lengths in order to protect their material assets. However, I am confident that all will agree that the value of our children by far exceeds that of any material possession. But oddly enough, many parents do not devote adequate time protecting their children from sexual abuse. This is due, in part, to all the confusion surrounding this subject. **Parents receive so much conflicting advice, usually from unqualified sources, that the line separating fact from fiction becomes blurred**. Oftentimes considering these principles that are not necessarily true can aid one in attaining a better understanding of those principles that are.

This section is designed to do just that by uncovering some of the most common misconceptions surrounding sexual abuse against children.

Misconception No. 1 - The Term Sexual Abuse

Many parents believe that in order to report someone for sexually abusing a child the abuser must carry out a complete sexual act with the child. This is absolutely not the case. **Any inappropriate action committed by an adult toward a child for the purpose of sexual gratification is considered sexual abuse**. An example could be someone merely exposing themselves to a child for sexual gratification. Such an event can and should be reported to the authorities.

Misconception No. 2 - It Can Never Happen to My Child

This thought happens to be the most common, as well as the most dangerous misconception. Parents not only think that sexual abuse only happen to other children, but that the odds are low of it happening to any child. The U. S. Department of Justice Office of Juvenile Justice states that there are more than 300,000 reported cases of sexual abuse against children each year. Recall that these do not include the thousands of unreported and undiscovered cases. **The F.B.I. goes on to state that one out of every four girls and one out of every six boys will be sexually abused by the time they reach adulthood**. Although your child may not fall into these statistics, it is important to realize that the first step to effectively protecting your child is to accept that "it can happen."

Misconception No. 3 - Studying This Subject Will Cause Paranoia

I will admit that there can be a fine line between being cautious versus being paranoid. When dealing with issues concerning our children, oftentimes we find ourselves on the extreme end. However, when talking about protecting our children from someone who might sexually abuse them, we should get just as close to that separating line as possible. It is difficult to believe that you can be "too" cautious when dealing with such an issue. The key to avoiding complete paranoia is by gaining proper knowledge, as well as wisdom concerning this subject. Knowledge meaning the understanding of safety principles and wisdom meaning the ability to apply that knowledge. **When you learn various safety principles and in turn learn how to put them into practice, it becomes more of a lifestyle rather than something you must think about continually**. This state of mind is commonly referred to, in karate terms, as a "relaxed sense of awareness." Getting past the thoughts of paranoia and understanding the value of applied knowledge truly leads to empowerment for both parents and children.

Misconception No. 4 - Adults Do Not Think of Children "That Way"

The words still ring in my ear of a mother whose son was the victim of sexual abuse when she said, "The thought that an adult could desire a sexual relationship with a child is something that never crossed my mind." The truth is that there are mentally disturbed adults who specifically target young children. In fact, the U. S. Department of Justice has reported that there are approximately four million known pedophiles in the United States. **While it is not necessary that we understand all there is to know about these people, it is vital that we realize that such people do exist**.

Misconception No. 5 - It Was a One Time Event

There have been many incidents where an adult has discovered sexual abuse against a child. When caught, the pedophile could demonstrate so much remorse that even the most critical adult may begin to feel compassion for him. One must quickly remember that the pedophile's life is built around secrecy and deceit. Regardless of the confessions from the abuser, he must be reported. Law enforcement and psychiatric studies lead to one mutual conclusion. **Pedophilia is a lifestyle, and the pedophile will, unless stopped, most likely abuse children continually throughout his entire life**.

Misconception No. 6 - I Would Know If My Child Was Being Hurt

Most children cry for their parents anytime that they are hurt. It doesn't take many years of parenting to discover kids often come crying, even when it is obvious that they are not really hurt (i.e., falling down and bumping their knee).

This leads parents to believe that their child would come to them if anyone were hurting him/her. Some of the various reasons children don't inform others that they are being victimized has been mentioned early in this section, but in addition to those, parents need to understand that often the children being sexually abused do not realize they are being hurt. As parents, we usually hear the term sexual child abuse and immediately assume that we are dealing with an adult who is violently abusing a child. While this can be the case, most often it is not. **Because the pedophile is seeking continual occurrences with a child, he tends to use various methods of persuasion rather than one violent act.** In fact, children, due to their innocence, often enjoy the attention they receive from the adult. Because the pedophile preys on a child's innocence and sense of trust in this area, it quickly becomes apparent just how much of a responsibility we have in protecting our children against sexual abuse. We cannot simply rely on children to tell us.

Misconception No. 7 - My Child Is Safe Because He Stays Away From Strangers

This happens to be another one of the common, as well as dangerous myths surrounding sexual abuse against children. While children are sometimes victimized by strangers, **nearly 90 percent of the time they are sexually abused by someone they or their parents know. That person may even be trusted and respected by both the child and family**.

Misconception No. 8 - Children are only sexually abused by adults

Obviously children's curiosity concerning one another's bodies is quite normal. However, as unsettling as it is, children can be and sometimes are sexually abused by older children. This does not imply that any time an older child shows interest or spends time with a younger child something improper is necessarily occurring. The key is that parents and children alike should be aware of an individual's behavior. **Regardless of their age or who they are, if a particular person's behavior causes concern, children should be kept away from that person.**

Misconception No. 9 - Older children are not vulnerable to sexual abuse

Many parents believe that as their children approach their teens, they are less vulnerable to sexual abuse. **The truth is that these older children can actually be more vulnerable.** In fact, the Federal Bureau of Investigation states that the largest percentage of reported sexual abuse cases consists of children between the ages of 11 and 17.

PREVENTION

It is obvious that we can never assure that our children are 100 percent safe from those individuals intent on doing them harm. However, as previously stated, there are many precautions we can implement that can assure that our children are safer. **Because sexual abuse can go undiscovered for weeks, months, or even years, we must do all we can to prevent such victimization against our children.** Above all, we must take a proactive approach. This section is designed for the sole purpose of providing practical steps that can and should be taken "now." While some of the tips will be self-explanatory, others may require a little more information in order to realize their importance. It is my hope that by understanding and applying the following principles, you can be confident that you are doing your part to protect your child from sexual abuse.

- **The Three S's (Umbrella Coverage)**
- **Know Everyone in Your Child's Life**
- **Teach Assertiveness**
- **Exercise Communication**

THE THREE S's (UMBRELLACOVERAGE)

It is important that we do not necessarily focus on any one particular safety tip at the expense of neglecting others. I consider all of the tips included in this program to be essential. **There is one strategy; however, which has proven time and again to be a very effective and efficient approach to preventing sexual abuse against a child.** Just as many people will choose one insurance policy that covers all of their personal needs rather than several individual policies, we can also take a similar approach to protecting our children. I refer to this "umbrella coverage" as the three S's: **self-esteem, self-confidence, self-awareness.** While these attributes may not guarantee that a child will never be a victim of sexual abuse, those children lacking in these areas appear to be the pedophile's primary targets.

-Self-Esteem-

Self-esteem can be summarized as a person's sense of self-worth. **One of the first traits that the pedophile looks for in a child is low self-esteem.** Quite often these children are easily persuaded to believe that no one really cares for them or what happens to them. More than anything else, children must know and truly feel that they are loved and valued. As adults, we need to assure children that their feelings are important, that their fears are important, and especially that they themselves are important. By devoting our time, our love, as well as our sincere attention to our children, we can assist greatly in this important area of emotional development.

-Self-Confidence-

Self-confidence allows children to take their sense of internal self-esteem and manifest outwards through actions. Confidence is primarily one's sense of self-reliance. Confident children develop a tremendous sense of empowerment. These children not only understand that they are important, as well as valued, but they are willing to take action against those attempting to convince them otherwise. **Those individuals who target children quickly recognize the confident child as a "hard target."** The pedophile most often avoids these children.

-Self-Awareness-

Self-awareness is a child's ability to be tuned to his/her own instincts. **Children who are abused almost always initially "feel" that something is just not right.** We need to teach children that when they have these confusing or "funny feelings" toward any individual or situation, they must inform us. Pedophiles know they will face this obstacle with most children, and through persuasion and persistence, they know they can usually overcome it. **By teaching children that those confusing feelings are actually a warning signal to danger, we can help them better understand how to respond to them.** Believe it or not, children's instincts often surpass those of even the most observant adults. It is vital that we teach our children how to, not only recognize their own instincts, but also respond to them.

KNOW EVERYONE IN YOUR CHILD'S LIFE

It is not my intent to lead one to believe that everyone who enters a child's life is trying to harm him/her. However, **I am of the opinion that assuming someone is guilty until "proven" innocent is an effective and necessary approach when concerning children**. It never ceases to amaze me, even with all of the information available today, how many parents still allow their children to be involved in various situations or events with other adults about whom they know virtually nothing. For example, parents will often allow children to spend the night with friends from school while knowing very little or nothing about their parents, or allow children to join sport teams and spend little time, if any at all, researching who their coaches might be. One of the most common responses parents state concerning such issues is, "If that particular adult were questionable we would have heard about it from someone." We must never lose sight of the fact that we are dealing with a "secret" crime. It has been stated that it is common for a pedophile to victimize as many as 150 children before he is ever caught. As with many principles concerning this issue, the following are not all inclusive; however, they do provide a strong foundation for identifying potential child predators.

-Behavior vs. Characteristics-

Many images tend to enter one's mind when attempting to conceive what the pedophile actual y looks like. Time and again it has been proven that the pedophile cannot be pointed out by any particular physical appearance. **However, there do appear to be a number of common behavioral traits that may define potential pedophiles**. It is important to note that the observances of these traits do not necessarily indicate that a person is a pedophile. These behavioral patterns simply provide us with a reference point from which we can work, in order to exercise our own judgment. Bottom line; it is essential to judge a person by his behavior more so than by any specific attribute. (Refer back to the "Enemy," and "How They Operate" section of this book to review some common behavioral traits of the pedophile.)

-References/Referrals/Backgrounds-

One of the most often overlooked areas of prevention against child victimization is the oversight of practical research into the lives of those involved with children. Though carrying out such measures may not necessarily point out that an individual has a specific past of abusing children, there may be a number of habitual behavioral habits, which could be of some concern. It should not make any difference whether you are dealing with teachers, scout leaders, coaches, instructors, babysitters, child care providers, or even hired laborers, etc. . . . **Anyone who has continual access to your child must be screened**. The process can be as simple as thoroughly investigating and verifying a person's given references and credentials. Even more elaborate measures can be taken by pursuing various authorized legal background checks through local or federal law enforcement agencies. Regardless of the method used, this process should "never" be overlooked.

-Trusting Your Intuition-

There is absolutely no substitution for that deep down "gut feeling" that parents possess. That inner alarm system is an example of how our subconscious reveals potential dangers to us that our conscious mind may not recognize. **Whenever our intuition signals to us that something could be wrong, something almost always is.** Regardless of behavior patterns, in the past or present, an individual that causes you "any" concern should not be allowed access to your child. In the event that a potentially questionable person is already involved in your child's life, he should be removed immediately. Your instincts should never be ignored.

Teach Assertiveness

It is important that we teach children to respect adults. However, it is even more important that they understand this should never come at the expense of compromising their own safety. **Children must be taught that if they feel their safety is a risk, it is acceptable for them to resist an adult,**

even if it means that they must be rude to that adult. Because the pedophile is usually very experienced and effective at persuasion, a child must be taught more than just how to say no.   One very effective principle is to teach children that it is "against the law" for anyone to abuse them. Children often do not understand the moral implications of sexual abuse, but even very young children understand basic legal situations.   For example, even preschool children understand that a red light means to stop, and to disobey that rule means you would be breaking the law. Breaking a law could in turn involve a ticket from the police. You can use the same basics to teach your child that it is against the law for an adult to do certain things to him/her.   It is reassuring for children to know that if someone abuses them that not only are parents concerned, but the police are as well. **It is the child who is willing to say no and mean it, as well as add that this is against the law, or say I am going to tell my mom and the police, which is truly exercising assertiveness.**

The following are additional principles that should prove beneficial in developing assertiveness.

-Who They Can Trust-

Odd as it may sound, telling children exactly who they can trust could be one of the most dangerous things an adult can do. When you inform a child that he/she can always trust a particular person, there are two potentially damaging things that can occur. First, from the child's point of view, you are telling him/her that anything that particular person does is acceptable. Secondly, you are denying the child the opportunity to exercise his/her own instincts. In such a situation, a child is being taught the very opposite of self-assertiveness.

-Forced Affection-

One of the most confusing issues for children to understand is forced - affection. How often are we guilty of telling our children it is okay to say no to an adult and then turn around and force them, against their will, to give Uncle Joe a big hug for his generous birthday present? Uncle Joe may be completely harmless, but that is really beside the point. **Teaching children that they have the right to refuse the affections of others, while forcing them to do just the opposite, only brings more confusion**. It is also important to note that forced affections are not limited to hugs or kisses, etc. . . . Forced affections can entail any form of attention, whether it is forcing a shy child, who may be trying to hide behind you, to step forward and speak with someone, or even something as innocently as grandma pinching his/her cheeks. Regardless of the situation, we should not force the issue.

-Physical Boundaries-

Many children understand the difference between appropriate and inappropriate touching, for example, an adult tucking a child's shirt in versus an adult doing so and obviously placing his hands in private areas. However, many more children are innocent in these areas and totally oblivious to such issues. Because the pedophile preys on a child's innocence, it is vital that you teach your child about specific physical boundaries. I am not of the opinion that young children must necessarily refer to their private areas in a correct anatomical fashion, but I do believe children need to be taught to be more specific than simply referring to them as their "privates." By doing so, a child can be more specific in telling you what someone may have done, but he/she can also be specific in telling someone "no" to inappropriate touching. **When a pedophile deals with a child who knows specifically that certain areas of his/her body are not to be touched, he sees that child as an educated child and will most often seek an easier target.**

COMMUNICATION

It is virtually impossible for sexual abuse to occur without secrecy. For this reason, it is extremely important that you teach your child the importance of sharing information with you. When discussing this particular issue, it should be noted that we are not merely talking about secrets, but we are also dealing with communication. Open communication is a key element in effectively protecting our children. It is obvious that this book deals primarily with how we can teach our children to be safer. Not only is it necessary that we share information with them, they must also feel that they can freely share information with us. Following are specific measures to assist parents in this area.

-No Bad Secrets-

The question quickly arises, what is a bad secret. The answer is basically any secret that in keeping, could bring about harm. The problem with teaching children this rule lies in the fact that many children are victimized while being persuaded that they are not actually being hurt. Therefore, it is beneficial to go a step further and teach your child that there are no secrets in your family. This should be especially emphasized when dealing with physical touching.

-Listen to Your Child-

The line of communication should always be open between you and your child. Children may be taught that they are not to keep secrets from you, but if you appear to be too busy or simply unwilling to devote time to listening to them you are guilty of placing your child at risk. When listening to your child, stop what you are doing and offer him/her your undivided attention. In addition to reassuring children we will listen to them, it is also essential that we learn how to listen. **Children seldom come right out and inform someone that they are being abused.** In addition to other reasons, children often do not know exactly how to explain what is happening. We must learn to recognize the clues. These clues can be verbal or even displayed through changes in a child's behavior or attitude. For example, your child may return from a sleep over party and say his/her friend's father tried to climb into his/her sleeping bag after everyone went to sleep. On the other hand, your child may return the next morning and say that he/she is "never" spending the night over at the friend's house again because his/her father is mean. It is apparent that both statements indicate that something happened at the sleep-over. However, the second statement is so subtle that it could be overlooked. Obviously, this second statement does not necessarily imply that your child was abused. He/she could have merely had an argument with his/her friend, where the father had to intervene. Nonetheless, when our children give us subtle clues, it is our responsibility to tactfully (without undue pressure) find out what is wrong. The bottom line is that we should always be prepared to address the obvious, as well as the subtle, communications from our children.

-Believe Your Child-

Children must feel that they can tell you anything, but they also need to know that they will be believed. Keeping in mind that children can misinterpret situations, it is not always advisable to prosecute someone based solely on information from a child. However, incident studies seem to indicate that most children, especially those who are able to explicitly describe their abuse, seldom make up stories concerning sexual abuse. Whether there appears to be adequate evidence or not, you should always respond to your child's report by separating him/her from the potential abuser. The bottom line is that, if your child informs you that he/she is being abused, you must absorb all of the information, encourage your child, and assure him of your shared concern. Then, as an adult, you can assess that information and pursue the proper actions.

-Affirmation-

As adults, we understand that demonstrating our love toward someone through actions speaks volumes, compared to merely saying the words "I Love You." However, it is important that we take a moment to reflect on the fact that we are dealing with children. Today it appears that most parents are so busy attempting to provide for their children with the nicest clothes, a nice home, a good education, etc., that they neglect what is most important to that child, and that is simply hearing the words, I love you. **While most children do not understand all that we do for them, they do understand that we love them when we verbally tell them**. Children who know that they are loved most often maintain a strong bond with their parents. Such a bond leads, not only to a closer family relationship, but also to better communication.

CHAPTER TWO

Sexual Abuse Check List

CHILD'S RESPONSIBILITY

☐ Understand and respond to your instincts, your "funny feelings"

☐ Be assertive about protecting your own body

☐ Never keep secrets from your parents, and always talk to them when someone makes you feel uncomfortable

TEACHER'S/EDUCATOR'S RESPONSIBILITY

☐ Reinforce parent's efforts by being concerned with the safety and overall development of the children you teach

☐ If a child confides in you concerning sexual abuse, you are required by law to follow your school's guidelines in reporting it to the proper authorities

☐ Promote your students self-esteem

PARENT'S RESPONSIBILITY

☐ Support your child's self-esteem and develop a confident child, tell him/her you love him/her

☐ Screen everyone who is involved in your child's life, and the first place to start is by observing their behavior

☐ Never force your child to trust someone or allow forced affection

Chapter Three

Child
Abduction

3

CHAPTER THREE

Child Abduction

Because the media covers only a handful of the highest profile cases each year, many believe that the occurrence of child abductions by strangers is rare; sadly this is not the case. The National Center for Missing and Exploited Children reports that there are approximately 4,600 children abducted by strangers each year.   While thankfully the majority of these children are safely recovered, many are not so fortunate. **I am sure that all will agree that if there was only one child abduction occurrence per year, regardless of whose child he/she is, that would still be one too many**. For that reason, it is vital that we do all we can to protect our children from this form of victimization.

Similar to the previous chapter, this chapter begins by defining abductions, describing the child abductor, as well as revealing how and why he does what he does.   The chapter continues by offering sound safety advice geared specifically for the prevention of child abductions, as well as separating fact from fiction, by covering common misconceptions concerning child abductions.

Defining Child Abduction

By definition child abduction is the removal of a child from an area, whether by force or persuasion, without the consent of that child's parent or supervising guardian.

THE ENEMY

Similar to the pedophile, the child abductor may not necessarily stand out in the crowd. While an abductor can be a family member or an acquaintance, our primary focus for this section will be the stranger abductor.

MOTIVATION

(Why They Do What They Do)

The child abductor's motivations can vary. Quite often, family or acquaintance abductions are carried out to create leverage against a parent or guardian. Of course there are also abductors who take a child for the sole purpose of financial gain through ransoms. There are also many cases where the abduction is brought about by emotional motivations, for example, a woman who desperately wants her own child. There are also many abductions that are committed solely for sexual purposes. Finally, there is, what law enforcement considers, the psychopathic child abductor.

These are the ones who take a child for the sole purpose of taking his/her life. Most often there is sexual abuse involved in such cases as well. Regardless of those involved or their motivations, child abductors are the worst level of criminals in our society.

METHODS

(How They Operate)

Many people hear the term child abduction and immediately have horrifying images enter into their mind. For example, one might have an image of a van pulling up to an unsuspecting child, snatching him/her up, and quickly driving away. Such situations have been known to occur, but most of the time the abduction is carried out through a much more subtle method. **The following are not all inclusive, but they do represent some of the most common "tricks of the trade" the child abductor may use to lure children from secure areas.**

-Bribery-

One of the most recognized and probably the one scheme most parents teach their children to avoid is bribery. The abductor may offer a child things such as candy or money to draw the child in close or even persuade the child to go with him somewhere (i.e., for a walk or a ride). **Many abductors have found this to be a very effective method, especially against young children.**

71

-Animals-

When it comes to animals, children can be extremely vulnerable. Whether it is allowing a child to pet their puppy, cat, etc., or trying to persuade a child to come over to their vehicle to see their pet. Abductors use animals to lure children from secure areas, so that their actions may be undetected.

-Assistance-

Abductors often prey on a child's desire to be helpful. They may ask a child to help them find a lost pet, carry packages, open a door or just simply ask for directions. **Either way, they are attempting to distract the child in order to take him/her**.

-Kindness/Trust-

Many times the abductor will overwhelm a child with kindness. **With a gentle look and persuasive conversation, an abductor can often build immediate trust with a child, while at the same time, looking for an opportunity to lure the child away from a secure area.**

-Authority-

A very common technique for the abductor is an attempt to exercise authority over the child. He may pose as an unknown family member, an employee in the store, or even a law officer. Either way, he will usually tell a child who he is and that the child must come with him. **He may even imply that the child's parents sent him to pick him/her**

up and take him/her home. A very common technique is for a potential abductor to inform a child that something has happened to his/her parents and that they are in the hospital. The abductor does this to place the child in a state of concern or panic. After doing so, he might inform the child that he was sent by the parent to pick him/her up.

MISCONCEPTIONS FACING CHILD ABDUCTION

Most often one will find that, where a specific area of safety is overlooked, misinformation is a contributing factor rather than neglect. The information, or in this case misinformation, given or implied to the public plays an essential roll in the overall attitudes and actions taken to combat various threats against children. It appears that the subject of child abductions is no exception. You may recall that, in order for a child predator to be effective, he must find or create an "opportunity" to victimize a child. Oddly enough, we often discover, based on our own actions, that we not only fail to do all we can to protect our children in this area, but we unknowingly place our children in vulnerable situations, creating the very opportunities that the child predator is searching for. Though the misinformation may be the culprit, rather than neglect, children are vulnerable nonetheless. The following are six basic misconceptions surrounding child abductions. **It is essential that you separate the fact from fiction in these specific areas, in order to assure that you are doing your part to protect your child from an abduction.**

Misconception No.1 - Abductions only occur in certain areas, only affect certain types of families, and cannot happen to my child.

Many think that child abductions only occur in high risk areas, such as the inner cities, where various other crimes may be prevalent. Most of these same people believe that child abductions only affect poverty-stricken families, or families who severely neglect their children. The truth is that child abductions have occurred in the inner cities, the suburbs, in the country, etc. . . . Child abductions can and have occurred in various families as well, regardless of race, income level, etc. . . . **The bottom line is that a child abduction can happen anywhere and to literally anyone.**

Misconception No. 2 - There are only a few child abductions per year.

Due primarily to the fact that media only covers what is considered the highest profile incidents, it appears as though the United States only encounters two or three abduction cases per year. Recall that the National Center for Missing and Exploited Children reports that there are approximately 4,600 non family child abductions reported to law enforcement agencies each year. **This means that, on average, not including family related incidents, there are more than 12 children abducted in the United States "every day."** While the largest percentages of children are returned home safely, many are returned severely injured, sexually abused and traumatized; others are found dead or never found at all. Looking past the media hype and into the real numbers behind this subject should truly be an eye opener for most everyone.

Misconception No. 3 - Family related child abductions are not serious.

How much harm can a child be in when being abducted by an immediate family member; after all, they are basically taking the child because they love him/her and want to care for him/her? This question is asked quite often, and as disturbing as it may be, whether motivated by custody battles or some other factor, many children who are abducted by a non custodial family member are in danger. In fact, the U. S. Department of Justice estimates that 80% of the children involved in such incidents are taken out of anger or revenge. Not only are these children traumatized, but often they are injured. **The bottom line is that child abductions involving a family member are oftentimes just as serious as an abduction by a stranger.**

Misconception No 4 - Most children that are abducted are actually only runaways.

The U. S. Department of Justice reports that there are approximately 450,000 runaways in the United States each year. When you compare these numbers with the number of abducted children, it is easy to see how mistakes can be made. **Though the numbers do vary, those incidents that are "reported" as abductions should always be treated as abductions.** Law enforcement agencies, as well as the media, work diligently to report incidents for what they truly are. Even with these efforts, oftentimes information is released to the public, describing as abduction case, while later discovering the child was actually a runaway. The point is that many missing children do turn out to be runaways; however, for the most part, those children "reported" as abducted are usually just that, abducted.

Misconceptions No 5 - Abductions are always extremely violent.

All child abductions traumatize those involved. However, most often, the actual taking of the child is seldom an initial act of violence. Many parents imagine a stranger running up to a child, grabbing them, and dragging them away as the child kicks and screams. Though this can occur, the most common abduction is quite the opposite. **True child predators learn quickly that in order to take a child and be undetected in the process, they must be much more subtle in their actions.**

Misconception No. 6 - Abductions only affect younger children

Many parents assume that child abduction only happen to small children. The truth is that the abduction can happen to a child of any age. In fact, a recent incident study conducted by the U. S. Department of Justice indicates that similar to sexual abuse, the greatest number of reported abduction incidents involve children between the ages of 11 and 17. Many times children in this age group fall into, what I refer to as, a protective gap. In other words, children in this age category have passed the stage where parents must watch everything they do. For example, the children in this age group know that they should not play with matches, run out in front of cars, or play with guns. Also, many in this age group have yet to reach the most difficult teen years, where they are on their own more and parents worry about them virtually every minute of the day. It is almost as if parents feel that they have brought their children through one difficult phase in life and have a few short years to catch their breath before the next difficult phase begins. For this reason, preteens and young teens can actually be more susceptible to abductions than younger children.

PREVENTION

Understanding how the potential child abductor will work is vital. But in addition to this, we must become educated in areas of prevention. If there was ever a subject that calls for the old cliché, "An ounce of prevention is worth a pound of cure," this would most certainly be it. **It is essential that we realize that there are some situations where the only logical remedy is avoidance**. Rather than go through life paranoid about everyone you see and whether they may be potential predators, you should learn basic preventive measures. Proactive techniques, when applied, can dramatically decrease the odds of your child falling prey to an abductor. The following are five categories containing specific prevention techniques.

- **Dealing with Strangers**
- **Home and Automobile Safety**
- **Public Safety**
- **School Safety**
- **General Safety**

DEALING WITH A STRANGER

One of the first questions I ask young people is, "How would you describe a stranger?" Without fail, the students begin describing someone mean and scary. They will often describe him with long ugly hair, missng teeth, and wearing dirty clothes. Though I never know my students personally when I speak to them, I have yet to have one raise their hand and point out that I am a stranger to them. This information should be quite disturbing due to the fact that the child abductor seldom looks as scary or dirty as the children describe. Most often he looks just as normal as you and me. Of course, we know that the child abductor is far from normal, regardless of how well you teach your child to apply the following "stranger" principles, if he/she does not understand who they apply to, they are useless. The first step, as well as the most important step for teaching children how to deal with strangers, is to help them understand that **A STRANGER IS ABSOLUTELY ANYONE THAT THEY DO NOT KNOW!** The following are five specific tips for dealing with strangers.

-Be Aware of the Tricks-

The first pages of this section include what we consider the "tricks of the trade" for the child abductor. **Because children are able to respond better to situations they recognize, it is essential that you devote adequate time**

to explaining such tactics to your child. Do recall that these tricks are not all inclusive; children should be taught to avoid anyone who attempts to trick or persuade them in any way (Refer to Methods, how the abductor operates).

-Keep a Distance From Strangers-

It is obvious that, in order for someone to attempt to harm a child, he must get close enough to do so. **Children should be taught to stay at least two steps away from anyone they do not know**. If some stranger approaches them, they should be taught to take at least two steps back and even run if necessary. (See Step back - Turn - Run on page 92)

-Do Not Accept Anything From a Stranger-

In an attempt to get a child close, as well as let his guard down, an abductor often offers something to the child. **It is vital that you teach your child not to accept ANYTHING from a stranger**. Even if the stranger may be holding something that belongs to the child (i.e., a child drops something and some stranger picks it up).

-Do Not Communicate With Strangers-

The child abductor (as the predator) is attempting to take a child (the prey). The first step of any predator is to effectively close the distance between him and his potential prey. The child abductor most often attempts to close the distance through communication. **Verbal or even nonverbal, by means of smiling and hand gestures, etc., the predator is attempting to distract the child in order to** get in closer. For this reason, children need to be taught that they should not carry on any communication (verbal or nonverbal) with anyone they do not know.

-Never Go Anywhere With a Stranger-

Children must be taught that, regardless of anything the stranger says, it is NEVER acceptable to go ANYWHERE with him. This not only includes getting into a vehicle or leaving a store, but also includes simply walking around a corner, or just outside of the yard.

HOME AND AUTOMOBILE SAFETY

Generally, one would consider his/her automobile or especially his/her home to be a safety zone. However, there have been cases where children have been removed directly from these places. **For this reason, it is important that you take the necessary precautions to assure that your child is not placed at risk in these two areas.** The following are steps that you can follow now to assist in protecting your child.

-Maintain a Secure Home-

Always follow sound home safety rules. For example, install solid deadbolt locks, keep your property well lit (especially motion lights around your home's exterior), and install storm windows. In addition to these, one of the most valuable investments you can make for the security of your home is a quality security system. Also, keep in mind that just to have one is not enough; you must learn how to operate it. **One final tip that is least practiced is to simply walk around your home as though you were trying to break into it. Look for vulnerable areas and address them appropriately.**

-Never Leave Young Children Unattended at Home-

As with so many other child safety issues, there is absolutely no substitution for adult supervision. **This not only includes the home itself, but also around the home.** Also, consider from a previous section the principle behind "active" supervision. Just to be present in or around the home may not be sufficient.

-Teach Children the Basics of Home Safety-

It is very important that children be taught that they, under no circumstances, answer the door, much less let someone into the house that they do not know. Children also need to be taught that, when they answer the phone, they should never carry on a conversation with someone they do not know. Teens, who may find themselves home alone, should be taught to never enter the house if something doesn't look right (i.e., an opened front door, broken glass, etc. . . .) These older children should also know that if someone were to call or come by looking for their parents, they should never reveal that they are alone; rather, they should always state that their parents are busy and unavailable. Finally, teach your child that if he/she ever feels threatened to dial 911, as well as call a trusted neighbor.

-Never Leave a Child Unattended in a Vehicle-

Leaving a child in a vehicle, even for a minute, can place that child at risk. Also, recall that distance can be important as well. For example, you place your young child in the vehicle and step away to replace a shopping buggy. **If you are more than 20 feet from that vehicle, someone could attempt to take your child, and it would be literally impossible for you to close that distance in enough time.** Whether you are parking at the front entrance to a store or parked in your own driveway, never leave a child unattended in a vehicle.

-Maintain a Secure Vehicle-

You do not have to see too many cases where a car jacking turned into a child abduction in order to understand the importance of basic vehicle safety. There have been situations where an individual has approached a vehicle, opened the door, and simply pulled out the driver in order to take the car, not knowing that there was a child in the back seat. For this reason, **ALWAYS, lock all of the doors immediately when you get into your vehicle, and keep them locked at all times.**

PUBLIC SAFETY

Keep in mind that we should not become overly paranoid. However, ask yourself this question, "Where would the potential child abductor mostly likely be found?" The answer is, "in the general public." Secondly, ask yourself the question, "Where would the child abductor find the greatest number of potential targets?" The answer is "in the general public." **While you should not necessarily be paranoid around the general public, it is important to realize that the general public is an environment in which we have very little control.** While you cannot dictate what occurs or who makes up the general public, there are some safety tips that can be implemented to assist one in maintaining control of your child's immediate surroundings.

-Never Leave a Child Unsupervised-

If your intentions were to catch a fish, obviously you would need to find water. It doesn't require much thought to realize that if you want fish, you must go to where they are. This is exactly how the predator (a child abductor) operates. **While an abductor may single his attention toward a specific child, more often he will go to areas where he will find more opportunities.** These predators will drive through the neighborhoods, walk through the parks, the malls (especially the arcades), even frequent youth centers and youth sporting events, all with the sole purpose of finding an unsupervised child whom they can target. For this reason, it is vital that you avoid leaving your child unsupervised in any public place.

-Protect Your Child's Name-

Though it may seem cute to have your child's name or nickname airbrushed or embroidered on his clothing, backpack or even bicycle tag, advertising your child's name (even verbally) in public can be very dangerous. **Nothing will cause even the most cautious children to let their guard down more quickly than to have someone approach them and call them by name,** while not realizing that the stranger just read the child's name on his/her shirt or heard his/her mother say it.

-Consider Specific Dress Codes-

How often have you observed your child playing with a group of children, only to have them blend together to the point that you must spend just a second to distinguish your child from the group? To avoid this occurring in public, consider dressing your child in something that you will recognize that is bright and colorful. **Also consider dressing your family in matching colored clothing when in large public places. This tip alone could help you quickly spot your child if you become separated.**

-Have a Lost Plan-

No matter how closely you watch your child, there is always the possibility that you could become separated. Rather than wait for such an event to occur, it is essential that both you and your child know what to do ahead of time. **Teach your child to look for an employee if lost in a store, and if he/she <u>must</u> ask a stranger for help, instruct him/her to approach a female, preferable one who is with a child. Most important, inform your child to never leave the area.** Assure him/her that if you were to ever become separated that you would never leave. As for the parents, the first step is to inform employees, as well as those around you. Many more reputable stores have a lock down policy. In the event some parent reports a child missing, the store gives an announcement over the intercom system describing the child; in addition, employees immediately monitor the exits, as well as parking lots, in an effort to locate the child. Secondly, always have an updated photo of your child with you to assist others in looking.

-Be Aware of Surroundings-

Whenever you or your child is in an unfamiliar environment or even in public places you have gone to your entire life, it is essential that you are aware of your surroundings. **Look for areas that may seem questionable and avoid such danger zones.** For example, a public restroom that is located next to a public entrance or exit should be considered such an area. If you allow your child to use this type of restroom, he/she could be vulnerable to someone who is waiting in or around that area to lure an unsuspecting child outside. Keep in mind that the predator seeks areas that will place odds in his favor, not only for spotting a child, but also successfully escaping with that child. While this is just one example, the bottom line is that, regardless of how busy you are or how much of a hurry you may find yourself in, always be aware of your surroundings.

SCHOOL SAFETY

Our schools, much like our homes, should be safety zones for our children. However, recall that the predator often spends time in areas where he is most likely to find an unsuspecting victim. For this reason, these are precautions that should be taken both in and around our schools. **Many of our schools today implement such steps, and if your child's school does not, I would encourage you to help the administrators see the importance of doing so.**

Also, if your child attends a school that is obviously understaffed, you should consider creating a volunteer program, where parents can rotate weekly or monthly to assist schools in these areas. What type of volunteer work could be more rewarding than contributing to the safety of our children?

-School Call Backs-

School Call Backs is a system, whereby principals require parents to call the school first thing in the morning, to inform them that their child will be absent. If a child is recorded absent during morning roll call and the parent has not called in, the school has a designated person who contacts the parents at home or work. **This system**

provides an effective method for assuring that a missing student has not been abducted, but is simply absent.

-Monitored School Access-

While parents do not want to feel they have limited access to their child, it is simply not safe to allow unlimited access into the school. **Once school is in session, there must be a monitoring process for all those entering and exiting the building.** Whether via video surveillance, audio screening, or even just having an office with an employee screening those who are entering or exiting, this is one area of school safety that must not be neglected.

-Monitored Child Pick-ups-

Similar to screening those coming into the building, **it is essential that schools implement an organized drop-off and pick-up system for all children.** Though this can be quite a task for larger schools, it is nonetheless a necessity. First and foremost, all schools should have separate areas for the younger grades (i.e., preschool - 3rd grade) to be picked up. Secondly, there should always be designated school workers monitoring these areas to assure all is well, and that these young students are not wandering around the school. Another valuable tip that is used most often on university campuses is to issue parents and students required window decals to assist in monitoring those driving around the school.

-Secured and Supervised Play Areas-

Regardless of the location of the play areas, all should be secure. **The most effective means for securing outside play areas is with perimeter fencing.** There is absolutely no excuse for any school to have an outside play area that is not fenced. Obviously, if someone wanted to climb a fence he could; however, such visual barriers prove to be very effective at, not only preventing children from wandering outside of designated areas, but also preventing others from easily coming in. **In addition to being fenced, these areas should be effectively supervised, with an adequate number of school workers.**

-Screening of All School Staff-

Whether considering authorized legal background checks through local law enforcement or having a designated person to thoroughly research and verify a staff member's references as well as credentials, **all employees working in and around a school must be screened (even temporary laborers and volunteers.).** Schools simply cannot allow questionable people to have access to our children.

Screening sample on next page

U. S. Department of Justice
Screening Sample

Basic Screening

☐ Employment reference checks

☐ Personal reference checks

☐ Personal interviews

☐ Confirmation of education

☐ Written application

☐ On-the-job observation

Intermediate Screening

☐ Local criminal record check

☐ State criminal record check

☐ FBI criminal record check

☐ State central child/development adult abuse registry check

☐ State sex offender registry check

☐ Nurses aide registry record check

☐ Motor vehicle record check

☐ Professional disciplinary board background check

Advanced Screening

☐ Alcohol/drug testing

☐ Psychological testing

☐ Mental illness/psychiatric history check

☐ Home visits

GENERAL SAFETY

Throughout this section, we have seen precautions and tips pertaining to parents, as well as children. **The following principles are a few of the essentials that I consider to be a child's sole responsibility.** You may recall that, while young children should share the least amount of responsibility for their safety, they do represent their last line of defense.

-Obey Parents-

Regardless of how effective specific safety tips are, if children do not obey them, they are virtually useless. Though it is definitely no excuse, children often fail to obey their parents because they fail to see the purpose for particular instructions. **Children must understand that the rules and guidelines given by parents are designed solely for the safety and protection of each child.** By disobeying their parents' rules, children can easily become vulnerable.

-Know Basic Personal Information-

Even the youngest child needs to learn specific personal and family information. Children should know both their own, as well as their parents' full names. In addition, children should be taught in early stages how to dial their own home phone number, as well as 911. It is also beneficial to teach a child how to use a public payphone, if necessary. **Children should learn these things but realize that this is private information that should not be shared with just anyone.**

-Walk Tall-

If there is any child that the typical child predator wants to avoid, it is the confident child. A child who walks with his/her head up and his/her posture in an upright position is demonstrating nonverbal communication. **The message being sent out is that he/she is confident and in control of his/her surroundings.** This outward demonstration, or "walk tall" attitude, can be very beneficial in preventing a child from being an easy target.

-Step Back *Turn *Run-

It has been stated that no particular tip or principle is more important than another. However, this one tip can be one of the most effective tips for any child. Whether discussing adult or child self-defense, controlling the distance between yourself and the perpetrator is vital. This quick mental/physical principle will assist a child tremendously in this area. Similar to the commonly known fire safety phrase, "stop-drop-and roll," children can be taught the personal safety phrase, **"step back - turn - and run."** In order for any predator to be effective, he must get close to his prey. **This action phrase is designed to teach children the principle of getting away from anyone they do not know.** In addition to this, children should yell. Merely yelling for help is not enough; what is important is that children must know how to yell the correct things. Rather than just run off screaming, the child needs to make specific statements. For example, "Help, this is not my parent. or this is a stranger." In doing so, a child has a greater chance of attracting the right type of assistance.

-Be a Tornado-

It is not very practical to assume that a small child can physically defend him/herself against an adult. This is exactly why this entire book places so much emphasis on prevention. However, in the event that an adult does attempt to take or harm a child, it is essential that the child knows how to escape. One of the most effective techniques for a child to use is a good old fashion temper tantrum. **Children should be taught to kick, scream, claw, bite, twist, and do everything possible in order to escape.** In other words, teach your child to be a "tornado" in the event some stranger actually does grab him/her.

CHAPTER THREE

Child Abduction Check List

CHILD'S RESPONSIBILITY

☐ Know the "tricks" child predators use

☐ Know personal information and contacts in the event you are separated from your parents

☐ Do not communicate, get close to, accept anything from, or go anywhere with someone that you do not know (step back - turn - run)

☐ Older children should know the rules for home safety, such as locking the doors and how to handle phone calls or visitors

☐ Always obey your parents' rules; they are for your own safety

SCHOOL'S RESPONSIBILITY

☐ Implement and maintain a student "call back" system

☐ Monitor all school campus access in and around the school

☐ Secure and adequately supervise all play or recess areas

☐ Monitor all child drop-off and pick-up points, and require that all students/parents/employees display specific school window decals or bumper stickers, etc....

☐ Screen absolutely all staff, including temporary workers, volunteers, and general project laborers.

PARENT'S RESPONSIBILITY

☐ Maintain a secure home and never leave young children unattended

☐ Never leave a child unattended in a vehicle for any reason

☐ Never allow your younger children to go unsupervised in public and always have a "lost plan" in the event you become separated

☐ Protect your child's name in public

☐ Always be aware of both you and your child's immediate surroundings

Chapter Four

Internet
The Information
Super Highway

4

CHAPTER FOUR

Internet
The Information Super Highway

More than 30 million young people log on every day to take advantage of the benefits offered by the Internet. Similar to so many other areas of technical advancements, the Internet is just one more example of how something very positive, can be distorted into something very negative. The Internet itself can be one of the most effective educational tools available to a child. It can be effectively utilized to research virtually every subject imaginable. While most experiences on the net are positive, there are potential risks to its users. The online world consists of a vast array of people. Most utilize the Internet for the good; however, there are those who use the Internet to victimize others, as well as conduct their own disturbed exploitations. **While there can be a number of dangers on the web, the two main concerns for young people are the risks of being exposed to objectionable materials and the risks of dealing with anonymous people.** The problem is that, due to the enormity of the web, it is literally impossible to "police" away these risks. The key is prevention. The good news is that through sound judgment, as well as the application of practical safety tips, Internet crimes against children can be preventable. This chapter provides you with practical tips, as well as clarification of basic misconceptions surrounding this subject. It is designed to assist you in educating your child concerning the potential dangers of the Internet, as well as assure you that your child is able to "surf" the net safely.

THE ENEMY

It is not the Internet itself that should be considered the enemy, but rather the twisted individuals who utilize the net as a tool to torment, entice, and literally entrap children. Recall that the child predator, in the purest form, does not wait for opportunities to victimize a child, but actually works diligently to create those opportunities. **These disturbed people have quickly found an effective medium for child victimization, through the Internet.**

MOTIVATION

(Why They Do What They Do)

While many of these disturbed people mentally torment children and families by sending out sexually explicit and/or violent material (i.e., child pornography), many more are using the Internet in an attempt to fulfill their own desires to sexually exploit children. Furthermore, **there are those who use the Internet in order to entice children to meet with them or to simply gain enough personal information so that they can find that child.**

The child predator's motivation for using the Internet is quite clear when you consider some of the basic requirements for successful child victimization. First of all, recall that, in order for the child predator to continually victimize a child, there needs to be secrecy. The Internet obviously offers this secrecy by the absence of visual contact, making it impossible to know exactly who the predators are. They can literally claim to be anyone, as well as any age. They can even claim to live in another part of the country, thus appearing to be no threat at all, when in reality they live in your own city. The ability to hide one's identity allows the predator the opportunity to gain a child's trust, which leads to the sharing of more personal information. Secondly, the predator needs opportunity. Due to the enormous number of children using the Internet, the child predator has approximately 30 million of these opportunities. The bottom line is that those who are seeking to harm children have discovered a very effective means to do so through the

Internet, and it is our responsibility to protect our children from those people.

METHODS

(How They Operate)

Many adults believe that someone communicating with their child through a computer does not pose an immediate threat. After all, their child is not out in public, but is safe at home, and the other person is most likely thousands of miles away. In fact, a child that is connected with someone on the Internet can even be more vulnerable than if that child were in public. The reason being is that while in public the average stranger will not know any personal information about your child. However, the skilled Internet user, through continued communication with your child, may know your child's name, age, address, and even the hobbies he/she enjoys and the school he/she attends. **Make no mistake; the child predator is quite skilled at coercing such vital information from young Internet users**. The following are some of the common ways the stranger gains, and maintains, communication with children.

- E-mail -

Many times the child predator will gain access to multitudes of e-mail addresses and randomly send out deceiving solicitations, in an attempt to get literally anyone to reply. For example, a child predator may send out messages claiming to have the special codes to a popular computer game, which will allow players to advance to higher levels. **A particular child may receive the message and reply**. This method of "baiting" is a common technique used by child predators to create a direct communication link with a child.

- Instant Messages -

Instant messaging is a form of interpersonal communication, whereby two people type live messages to one another, just as if they were speaking to each other by phone. The child predator uses this form of communication in an attempt to gain specific personal information from a child, while at the same time concealing his own true identity. For example, a predator may pose as a 13-year-old who loves computer games. He will use instant messaging to communicate with a child often enough that he begins to develop what appears to be a trusting relationship with him/her. **This process may even go on for days or weeks and eventually lead to an arrangement for an off-line person to person meeting**. It is only after this meeting that the child discovers the person he/she has been communicating with is actually an adult. The child predator also uses instant messaging to test a child with very subtle improper solicitations. For example, he may get a child deeply involved in a conversation and then tactfully introduce improper language or insinuations. This may be done to spark a child's curiosity or even test a child to get an idea of how far he/she will go. Most often it is used to slowly and tactfully get a child to remove boundaries between himself and the predator.

- Chat Rooms -

Chat rooms are areas on the Internet where people with common interests can enter and, via typed messages, communicate as a group in real-time. **Child predators use such tools in order to communicate with unsuspecting children, while being able to disguise their true age, name and where they live. Most of all, the child predator can hide his true intentions.** Oftentimes, a predator will frequent various chat rooms as a way of establishing a relationship with children in what appears to be a safe "group" setting. Sometimes he will deceive children into believing he is a child himself, and by coincidence, share the same interests. Other times, the predator may be more aggressive and introduce objectionable (sexually explicit) material in a chat room, anticipating that someone, whether for curiosity reasons or otherwise, will take the bait. Like instant messaging, child predators utilize chat rooms to first establish a relationship through continued communication. Secondly, the predator seeks to exchange information and/ or photographs, and often attempts to arrange an off-line "in person" meeting.

- Children's Web Sites -

As disturbing as it may sound, there are many child predators who create and operate their own personal Web sites. **While some may be quite explicit concerning their exploitations of children, others are disguised as child safe sites, catering to the interests of various age-groups.** Regardless of the type of site, the predator uses these as another means for establishing direct lines of communication with children, as well as gathering personal and private information.

MISCONCEPTIONS FACING THE INTERNET

The first step to understanding any particular area of personal safety is to clear up possible misconceptions surrounding that issue. Many parents do not devote time to educating their children about the potential dangers on the Internet. The primary reason that this area of child protection is so often overlooked is that most parents simply fail to understand just how vulnerable a child can be online. **It may sound surprising, but there are many adults who do not realize exactly what is accessible on the web**. At the other end of the spectrum are parents who are fully aware of the explicit information, as well as photos that are available. These parents tend to believe that the best defense against such exploitations is to avoid the Internet all together. The following are three misconceptions that every parent should avoid when considering their child's safety on the information super highway.

Misconception No. 1 - Denied Access

Many parents believe that the key to protecting their child is to simply deny them access to the Internet all together. Though it may appear that this is a practical solution, taking such measures will only deny a child the ability to use one of the most effective learning tools available. While there are many bad things on the web, as well as many nonfactual so called "expert opinions," there is also a wealth of knowledge that can be gained through this medium. For example, children have access to entire world wide encyclopedias, dictionaries, various interactive learning aids, and the list goes on and on. **The point is that denied access to the Internet is most likely not the answer.** When handled properly, the Internet can offer children a safe educational experience.

Misconception No. 2 - The Internet is 100% safe

There are some people who do not realize that the Internet can be a very dangerous place. I cannot tell you how many parents I have spoken with who thought that their child was safe because, after all, he/she is not doing anything but spending time in his/her room working on the computer. These parents never realized that their child was being exposed to subjects such as cult groups, anonymous people, as well as an array of explicit sexual exploitations. The truth is that the Internet is not 100% safe; it is far from it. **Because the information super highway is such an open medium, it is virtually impossible to regulate exactly who uses it and what type of material people display.** For this reason, it is essential that you teach your child how to approach it safely and responsibly. Though there is objectionable material out there, with the proper precautions and good moral judgment, it is possible to avoid having such material come into your home.

Misconception No. 3 - My Child Knows Not to Go to Specific Areas

It does not require very much time on the Internet to realize how easy it is to access objectionable material. What is so disturbing is that oftentimes such material seems to find you. It is quite common to be searching on the web for specific information, only to have objectionable material appear on your screen. **The National Center for Missing and Exploited Children states that there are approximately 30 million children using the Internet today, and one out of every four of these children will receive some type of sexually explicit material.** The point is that whether looking for it or not, there will always be improper material placed on the Internet, and you must take the necessary precautions to protect your child.

PREVENTION

The Internet can obviously be a valuable educational tool. The Internet can represent a potential danger zone as well. In addition to the objectionable material that children can be exposed to, there is also the danger of communicating with anonymous people. The child predator has quickly realized that, through the anonymity of the Internet, he can effectively create a connecting link to unsuspecting children. It is estimated that one out of every four children receive sexually or violently explicit material, and approximately one out of every five children on the

Internet receive solicitation to engage in some type of sexual engagement. **The challenge we face is to allow our children to take advantage of the Internet and the technology if offers, while at the same time working diligently to keep them safe.** The following preventive tips are offered to help you meet such a challenge.

- **Internet Familiarization**

- **Protecting Personal Information**

- **Avoiding the Danger Zones**

- **Exercise Supervision**

- **Install Filtering Devices**

PARENTS SHOULD BECOME FAMILIAR WITH THE WEB

It is surprising to discover the number of adults who have yet to take advantage of the technology offered by the Internet. **Familiarizing yourself with the net will not only provide you with access to a wealth of useful information, but can also assist you in protecting your child.** Though the Internet can be a dangerous environment for children, there are a number of safety measures available to help protect them while online. Whether via books, study courses, or even personal instruction from family or friends, the first step to implementing safety measures is to learn the basics of the Internet yourself.

PROTECTING PERSONAL INFORMATION

The Internet obviously offers users a tool for gaining information, in addition, the Internet serves as a very effective and efficient means for interpersonal communication. This interactive communication is not necessarily dangerous. **However, the problem arises with the ability others may have at intercepting given information.** In other words, oftentimes, information provided over the Internet is not secure and can therefore fall into the hands of literally anyone. Secondly, there are the child predators who utilize the Internet to target children in an attempt to acquire specific personal information. For reasons such as these, it is vital that you teach your child to avoid placing "any" personal information on the Internet (i.e., name, age, home address, phone number, e-mail, school's name, photos, etc. . . .)

AVOID POSSIBLE DANGER ZONES

It should be somewhat obvious that anything so enormously scaled and uncontrollable as the Internet, would pose its share of threats toward children. It has been estimated that there are more than 15 million Web sites found on the net that contain objectionable material unsuitable for anyone, much less children. Recall that in addition to being exposed to such material, there is also the threat of communicating with anonymous Internet users. **Whether via instant messages, chat rooms, or even unsolicited e-mail, child predators have quickly learned to utilize the anonymity of the Internet to create a connecting link to unsuspecting children.** Though there are many disturbed people who gain satisfaction by merely mentally victimizing children through inappropriate messages or photos, there are those on the web who make contact with children in an attempt to earn their trust, so that they can in turn set up an off-line face to face meeting with a child. For example, someone in a chat room who claims to be a 12-year-old boy interested in collecting baseball cards may actually be a disturbed adult who is attempting to persuade your child to meet him at the local mall or hobby shop. **Though the Internet is often used and was actually invented for interpersonal communication, I am of the opinion that, for a child's safety, it may be best that he/she avoids using the Internet for such purposes.**

Teach your child to avoid the various Internet danger zones. Teach your child that he/she is to "never" respond to unsolicited messages on the Internet. Above all, it is critical that you teach your child to "never" set up an in-person meeting with someone online. Taking such measures may seem harsh to some, but keep in mind that child predators often use these Internet resources as just another method for targeting vulnerable children.

EXERCISE SUPERVISION

Obviously you would not allow your child to roam unsupervised among millions of people you do not know. **While a child may not necessarily be physically roaming around in public, the dangers can be just as great while roaming around unsupervised on the Internet.** Today's children may appear to be much more mature than in days past, but they are still children. Whether through curiosity, peer pressure, or even the allurement of strangers on the web, children oftentimes find themselves exposed to harmful material, as well as potentially dangerous situations. For this reason, it is essential that you closely monitor and supervise your child's Internet activities. In addition, it can be quite beneficial to set designated times, as well as time limits for your child's Internet access. If necessary, you can program passwords that can "lock" your computer, thus enabling access without your knowledge. It should be noted that children are most vulnerable when they are bored and find themselves simply roaming through various Web sites. Setting up designated time limits teaches your child the principle of quality use versus quantity. The bottom line is that nothing can help assure that your child is safe on the Internet more than adult supervision.

INSTALLING FILTERING DEVICES

It may not always be practical to supervise all of your child's Internet activities. In such cases, filtering systems are by far the next best option. Filtering systems are basically software packages, which literally "block" out any areas containing objectionable material. **Modern filtering systems have become so advanced that they can literally monitor and control every aspect of your family's Internet activities.** Though many Internet providers are beginning to implement various filtering systems, it is possible to purchase and customize your own.

Many advanced filtering systems can even be programmed separately for each Internet user in your family. They can be programmed for a designated log on time, as well as set time restraints. While they are not 100% fool proof, they can be effective at blocking almost anything that a parent would consider unsuitable for children. Not only can these systems block what comes into your computer, but they can also be programmed to block various information going out of your computer. For example, filters can be programmed so that your child is unable to enter in or send any personal information through the web. Many systems can even be programmed to prevent children from conducting person-to-person communication, thus only allowing children access to games and research, etc.... Best of all, many of these advanced filters keep a literal internal diary of every activity your child engages in while online. This allows you to go in and review your child's Internet use to assure that the places he/she is going are "child safe." **Though I will be the first to agree that children need some privacy, it should "never" come at the expense of their personal safety.** To help reassure that your children are safe online, consider utilizing Internet filters.

CHAPTER FOUR

Internet
The Information Super Highway

CHILD'S RESPONSIBILITY

☐ Never place any personal information on the Internet, not even your age, where you go to school, or what city you live in

☐ Never respond to objectionable material or unsolicited messages, and always report these incidents to your parents

☐ Understand the risks involved concerning communication with strangers through the Internet, avoid all of the danger zones, AND NEVER agree to meet with anyone from the Internet

SCHOOL'S RESPONSIBILITY

☐ Reinforce parents' instructions by teaching the basics of Internet safety

☐ Supervise children's Internet access in class

☐ Utilize filtering devices and/or services

PARENT'S RESPONSIBILITY

☐ Familiarize yourself with the Internet

☐ Exercise supervision and review your child's Internet activities

☐ Utilize filtering devices, but also teach your child how to exercise good moral judgment

Chapter Five

School
Bullying

5

CHAPTER FIVE

School Bullying

Bullying is an everyday occurrence in the lives of thousands of children in the United States each day. For many, every day of school is nothing short of a nightmare. **In fact, the U.S. Department of Justice states that approximately 160,000 students skip schools every day due to the fear of being bullied.** Furthermore, almost 20 percent of students in school avoid using the restrooms and various other areas at school for the same reason. Bullying is definitely nothing new; however, due in part to vast media exposure, bullying is becoming one of the most dominant social issues of our time. Society is just now beginning to understand the potential damage that can be caused from exposure to persistent bullying. **Oddly enough, it is not only the victim who can suffer; the bully himself can face long-term repercussions as a result of his actions as well.** This entire section is designed to shed some light on the issue of bullying and offer specific steps that can be taken to help put a stop to such incidents, for the sake of all those involved.

Define Bullying

The broad definition of bullying is basically the act of harming or taking advantage of someone who is weaker. More specifically, the act of bullying consists of and is not limited to any act whereby one may abuse another, whether it may be physically, mentally, or emotionally for the sole purpose of harming that person **(For example, bullying can include striking another child, persistent name calling, teasing, threats of violence, exclusion, etc....)**

THE ENEMY

There is no set profile for a bully. Additionally, it is somewhat disturbing to literally think of a specific child who may very well be a bully just as the enemy. Therefore, rather than look at a specific individual, **bullying itself should be considered the enemy**.

MOTIVATION

(Why They Do What They Do)

The motives behind bullying vary. While bullying can be brought on by something as simply as one's jealousy toward another or even by the stereotypical "big kid" who takes lunch money from the "little kid," most often the habitual bully is driven by other motivations. The following are some of those dominating factors, which often lead children to bully other children.

- Lack of Parental Control/Involvement -

Children who are undisciplined by their parents will oftentimes assume the roll of a bully. These children, due to lack of behavior restraints at home, understandably exercise this behavior outside of the home. **Basically, these children often get what they want by "pushing" other kids around, simply because they are accustomed to "getting away" with it.** Bully-type behavior can also be attributed to lack of parental involvement. Many children, who live in an environment that lacks parental involvement, or who live in what may be considered an "emotionally cold" home, exercise this type of negative behavior, simply to receive attention from parents who, under normal circumstances are disconnected and not concerned with their child's normal activities. These children come to the conclusion that "negative attention" is better than no attention at all.

-Home Violence-

Oftentimes you will find that one who bullies is simply acting out what he/she experiences at home. **Many times these individuals are either bullied or exposed consistently to family violence in their own home.** These children may also come from homes with very little parental supervision and/or involvement.

-Bullied by Other Kids-

A bully can literally be, in some form or fashion, a victim of bullying himself. A bigger kid may victimize a child, so that child in turn releases his own frustrations by victimizing someone smaller or weaker than himself. **Bullying others appears to give back some sense of "control" that is lost when he is the victim.**

-Peer Pressure-

Peer pressure can also be a contributing factor concerning bullying. For example, a school may have one or many particular kids who appear to be the targets for negative attention. Those kids get picked on by literally everyone. **Many times a child will allow other kids to persuade him/her to follow suit and pick on the child as well, thus becoming "part of the crowd."**

-Fear of Being Bullied-

A child in his/her own mind may become a bully simply to prevent himself from being bullied. Many times, the one who stands up for the one being bullied soon finds himself being bullied as well. **Also, a child may take on the roll of a bully, in order to put on the appearance of the so-called tough kid, in an attempt to prevent others from bullying him/her.**

-Low Self-esteem-

Though there appears to be a multitude of exterior factors motivating bullying, the foundation of most all bullying is low self-esteem. For the child with low self-esteem, there are usually two avenues one can take. The first is to become overly introverted, shy and actively portraying the roll of a helpless victim. The second is to act out some type of negative activity in an attempt to "prove something" to others as well as himself. This appears to be one of the primary driving forces behind habitual bully-type behavior. **This child will utilize the sense of control, as well as the attention or notoriety he gains from victimizing others, in an attempt to feel empowered himself.**

-Extremely Violent-

Whether brought on by a deficiency in social skills, a child's inabilities to exercise logical conflict resolution, or having a problem with anger management, **there are some children who bully as a result of anger or even rage.** While such cases are not as common as the others, they can be the more serious ones.

METHODS

(How They Operate)

There are many different methods, whereby one child can bully or persecute another child. While the following is not necessarily an exhausted list of methods used by bullies, it should offer insight into some very important truths concerning this subject. **Primarily, this section brings to light the fact that bullying does not always involve a child physically striking another child.**

-Physical Intimidation-

The fact that a child may be bigger, stronger or more aggressive than another particular child is often a tool used by bullies to intimidate their victims. Though they may really never have any intentions of physically harming their victim, they remind them quite often that they are capable of doing so. **An example could be the stereotypical big kid making the smaller kid give up his seat or his lunch money**.

- Physical Abuse -

Physical abuse is obviously the act of bullying, whereby one child physically strikes another child. Though there are extreme incidents where a bully persistently "beats up" his victim, **most often, this type of bullying consists of day to day pushing, slapping or taking things**.

-Psychological Intimidation -

Mental intimidation is basically a bully tactic, whereby the bully preys on his victim's fear of the unknown. **Though he may never actually do anything to the other child, he is constantly threatening to do so**. An example could be a child continually telling another child that he is going to beat him up if he sees him after school or catches him in certain areas. This type of activity allows the bully to get into his victim's mind, in order to continually torment him.

- Social Intimidation -

Social bullying is basically nothing more than constant verbal "teasing." Society often implies that people should look, act, or dress a certain way. **Children who fit these certain social molds often tease others who may not.** Examples could be teasing someone who is over weight, too skinny, wears glasses, is poor, or even too rich, etc. . . .

- Exclusion -

Exclusion is just a higher level of social bullying. Oftentimes, children, who may be insecure themselves, form various school social groups or "clicks." Keep in mind that children who form their own groups or circle of friends are not necessarily bullying others simply because they don't include children who may not have common interests or hobbies. **Such groups basically become bully type groups when they not only alienate someone, but also make it quite obvious that they are excluding that particular person.** A simple example could be students in a class constantly alienating a new class member, by purposely ignoring him/her and excluding him/her from various class functions.

- Rumoring -

Though not thought of as a typical bullying situation, rumoring for a child can be a very tormenting experience,

125

especially for girls. **Children often spread terrible rumors about another particular child in an attempt to encourage others to treat that child differently**. This type of bullying has a tremendous emotional impact on that child.

MISCONCEPTIONS FACING BULLYING

It is obvious that bullying is at the center of today's social issues. However, even with all the talk about this subject, many adults have yet to pursue efforts to reduce the occurrences of child bullying. Similar to various safety issues, due to the misconceptions, as well as misinformation many receive little is being done concerning this subject. This section is designed to address five common misconceptions surrounding child bullying.

Misconception No. 1 - Kids Will Be Kids

This is, by far, one of the most common attitudes adults have when dealing with children bullying other children. **Many believe that bullying is just a fact of life, and children are very resilient**. In fact, some feel that this is nothing more than a child's way of establishing a general type of social pecking order — the strong survive. It is not my intent to indict those who fail to understand the seriousness of bullying; however, the aforementioned attitude should be absolutely unacceptable. The sooner all adults realize that bullying cannot be ignored as mere child's play, the closer we will be to a solution for this issue.

Misconception No. 2 - Bullying is Only Physical

Many fail to realize that bullying does not necessarily have to include physical abuse. Bullying can range anywhere from constant name calling, teasing, alienation, and exclusion to persistent physical threats. While verbal abuse inflicts no physical injury, the psychological impact can be just as harmful. **The emotional scars that often accompany "non provoked" verbal abuse can run deep, as well as last well into adulthood.** Whether physical or verbal, any type of persistent aggression carried out between children, should be addressed.

Misconception No. 3 - Bullying Only Affects Boys

While the percentage of physical attacks on girls is much lower than that of boys, girls are definitely not immune to bullying. **Though girls do sometimes physically bully each other, most often their abuse is nonphysical.** Like boys, the verbal teasing, alienation, or even the act of spreading rumors can have a long-lasting effect on the psychological development of girls. The point is that, like boys, girls can be equally affected, as well as involved in bullying.

Misconception No. 4 - Bully Labeling

It would not do this subject justice if we failed to consider the process of bully labeling. **Not "all" verbal or physical abuse can be labeled as bullying.** Often, you may witness a specific situation and consider only one aspect of that situation. For example, you may witness someone persistently teasing your child and immediately assume the other child is a bully, only to realize later that your child had previously provoked an altercation. Don't misunderstand, no one literally asks to be victimized or tormented by a bully. However, it is essential that you first assess incidents, in order to distinguish between provoked versus unprovoked situations.

Misconception No. 5 - The Bully is Unaffected

Many parents, both mothers and fathers, witness their own child exercising bully-type behavior. Many of these parents have the attitude that at least my child is not "being" bullied. While it appears the bully is getting the better end of the deal, this can be deceiving. **What few often realize is that the bully himself will often develop the same long-lasting characteristics as his victims**. For example, many bullies will eventually reach a stage in life where they can no longer push other people around. Once they are faced with the reality that they can no longer take advantage of others, many times those individuals become withdrawn, antisocial, and have developed even lower self-esteem. At the other extreme, there are those who exercise bully behavior throughout their entire lives, often leading to delinquent and even criminal behavior. The point is, the prevention of bullying is, in the long run, beneficial, not only for the victim, but the bully as well.

PREVENTION OF BULLYING

Making the statement that kids can be cruel is truly an understatement. Kids can be "very" cruel. Whether attributed to a lack of parental involvement, the need for effective roll models, or the explicit exposure to extreme violence via media and/or video games, etc., many of today's youth appear to be much more violent than in years past. In addition, those same children seem to possess an almost dulled sense of conscience, as well as remorse. **The fact is that we no longer live in a society where acts of bullying can be ignored**.

It becomes quite clear just how serious the bullying issue is once we begin to uncover some of the long-term effects it has on its victims. Various incident studies have shown that many children, who are subjected to persistent bullying, perform lower academically, have lower school attendance, have low self-esteem, and many develop a deficiency in various social skills. Additionally, some victims develop anxiety, depression, and even suicidal tendencies. Oftentimes these tendencies, as well as others, carry on well into adulthood. Persistent bullying can, in extreme cases, also lead to outward acts of violence (i.e., extreme school violence).

A recent government agency incident study revealed that nearly two thirds of all targeted school violence occurrences (shooting, bombings) were committed by children who complained that they were persistently bullied to the point of near torment. While such incidents are quite

129

rare, they do occur.

It is important to note that not all children who are bullied develop the various characteristics or violent tendencies just described. In fact, the vast majority will not. However, there is absolutely no way to determine that children will or will not be permanently affected. For this reason, it is essential that we do all we can to prevent the continuation of bullying. The following pages describe various measures that can be utilized to combat child bullying. These preventive responsibilities are divided between parents, schools, and children, in order to present the most effective, as well as efficient, approach for bully prevention.

- **Parent's Responsibility**
- **School's Responsibility**
- **Children's Responsibility**

PARENT'S RESPONSIBILITY

You may recall that parents share the largest responsibility for the personal safety of their children, and bullying serves as no exception. The prevention of bullying actually poses as a twofold responsibility. **It is the parents' responsibility to assist their children in various areas of development, and to help prevent them from being bullied by other children. Equally important is the fact that parents also have a responsibility of assuring that their child is not a bully.** In fact, society is beginning to implement accountability measures for parents whose children are involved in delinquent behavior (i.e., required family counseling and even criminal charges against parents whose children commit various crimes). The point is that we have seen that bullying can have a profound negative effect on all of those involved. For this reason, it is essential that parents do their part to combat child bullying. The following are specific principles that parents can utilize to not only prevent their child from being bullied, but also from being the bully.

"Preventing Your Child From Being Bullied"

-Promote Self-esteem -

Many children, for various reasons, simply do not feel good about themselves. Obviously, almost every child reaches a point in adolescence where he/she feels insecure about something. However, some children allow these insecurities to overcome them to such a degree that they not only fail to exercise outward confidence, but also lose all sense of self-worth. While these children may, at times, be singled out and bullied, often they are merely subjected to the same basic teasing and jesting that most experience. **The problem is that these children, with low self-esteem, seem to take such incidents extremely personally**. For example, there may arise a situation at school where a group of older kids passes by and make teasing remarks toward a group of younger kids. To many this may not be a big ordeal, but a child with very low self-esteem singles himself out by taking the incident as a personal attack. The point is that these children allow things to bother them so much that they assume the roll of a defenseless victim, in other words, an "easy target" for a bully.

The first key to promoting a child's self-esteem is through encouragement. So often we find ourselves overlooking the positive things our children do (i.e., good grades, good behavior, and even special talents). We take for granted that children should do these things and usually fail to offer them the praise they deserve. It is the parents' responsibility to not only praise their children for obvious reasons, but to look for or even create situations in which a child can gain praise and encouragement. Secondly, you can promote your child's self-esteem, simply by devoting your time to him/her. **"Nothing" encourages a child more than having caring parents who are willing to stop what they are doing and talk or especially listen**. Remember that most all children are going to be faced with insecurities in life and bullies often prey on these insecurities. The children with high self-esteem are going to work through their insecurities and are much less likely to fall prey to such victimization.

- Open Communication -

Most will agree that one primary factor that leads to a child being constantly bullied is low self-esteem. There are few elements that suppress a child's self-esteem more than the inability to share his/her problems and concerns with a trusted adult. It appears that most parents have a difficult time communicating with their children at any age, but especially as children approach adolescence years. What many parents fail to realize is that open communication does not just manifest itself. **In order to effectively communicate with your child, you must continually cultivate a relationship with him/her.** In other words, open communication only comes as a result of a trusting and healthy relationship between you and your child. Just as in promoting self-esteem, simply devoting your time to your child is a key factor in developing open communication.

This type of communication assures your child that he/she can always come to you with his/her problems, fears, and concerns. This gives you an opportunity to address certain issues in your child's life, so you can offer him/her encouragement, thus promoting self-esteem. Also, children who know they can openly communicate with their parents are more likely to inform you if something, or in a case of bullying, someone is bothering them. This allows you to intervene whenever necessary, to assist in diffusing potential problems before they become major conflicts. For example, if someone is targeting your child and your child informs you of the incident, you are then able to assess the situation from the onset, thus preventing it from escalating. The point is, exercising open communication between you and your child not only creates a stronger bond, but also contributes greatly to his/her overall development, as well as safety.

- Teaching Assertiveness -

Though children must learn the importance of being respectful and considerate toward others, they must also learn how to stand up for themselves. **Most often, the bully picks on certain children, because he/she knows these children will do nothing to defend themselves**. In other words, a stereotypical bully may take another child's lunch money simply because he/she knows he/she can get away with it.

One of the most common inquiries from concerned parents is whether or not they should teach children to stand up to bullies, by physically fighting them. This is a very pertinent question — and rightly so. The initial answer to this question is a resounding NO! There are very few, and I emphasize the words "very few," incidents that call for physical altercations. First and foremost, though verbal abuse can be equally as damaging as physical strikes, this type of bullying should never provoke physically striking the person initiating such abuse. If a child is the victim of physical abuse, his/her primary objective should be to get away from that person and seek the assistance of a trusted adult. Adults and children alike must understand that physical violence only compounds a problem. Such actions can and often do lead to permanent physical injuries, as well as legal actions. **The bottom line is that when you teach your child to be assertive, you are not necessarily encouraging him/her to fight the bully. Rather, you are teaching him/her that when faced with a bully, he/she should stand up for him/herself and let the bully know that his/her actions are unacceptable.** In the event that a child is unable to resolve the situation alone or if he/she is facing physical bullying, he/she must be assertive enough to involve a trusted adult.

"Preventing Your Child From Being the Bully"

-Lead by Example-

It has been stated that children will almost always mimic the behavior they witness from their parents. This certainly doesn't imply that all bullies are acting out negative behavior that they witness at home; however, this is often a factor. Some children do witness parents who are disrespectful to each another, as well as to others. Other children may live in an environment that appears uncaring or emotionally cold. In either case, many children who witness these types of behaviors, regardless of what they are taught, do demonstrate bully-type behavior, when around other children. On the other hand, a child who is taught sound family values, and also witnesses such behavior at home is less likely to attempt to bully or take advantage of others. **As simple as this sounds, many parents live by the rule, "Do as I say and not as I do." This is by no means the most effective way to approach bullying or any issue for that matter.** The point is that the most effective way to assist a child in any area of development, especially areas concerning the treatment of others, is to lead by example. It is the parents' responsibility to assure that their child develops strong moral character, and the most effective way to do so is for parents to exercise such character themselves.

-Promote Self-esteem-

A common characteristic that is most often shared between bullies and their victims is low self-esteem. Often you will find that bullies have such low opinions of themselves that they choose to bully others in an attempt to boost their own confidence. Most often, bullies do not necessarily get the significant boost in confidence that they are seeking when they initially bully someone. It is this very reason that often leads to habitual bully-type behavior. Though the bullying incidents themselves do not necessarily bring gratification, the attention and notoriety gained often do. One very effective method for promoting self-esteem, especially when attempting to encourage a bully to change his behavior, is what I refer to as "redirecting." **"Redirecting" is a method, whereby parents acknowledge a child's negative behavior and seek to not only eliminate that behavior, but go a step further and replace that behavior with something positive.** Many habitual bullies have no hobbies, activities, or specific attributes in which they can take pride. Offering them, such options can often have a profound effect. For example, you can encourage your child to get more involved in sports, academics, or community service, and the list goes on and on. Overall, promoting a child's self-esteem is not only a key element in his/her overall development, but also assists in the prevention of bullying.

- Discipline Your Child -

Obviously children need discipline. A young child, who snatches a toy away from another child or strikes a child out of anger and receives no punishment for such behavior, soon comes to the conclusion that this type of behavior is acceptable. For this reason, **it is essential that parents teach their children, at a very young age, that there are consequences to their actions, and that certain types of behavior will not be tolerated**.

While older children may be past the "snatching toys" stage, they still need discipline nonetheless. Believe it or not, children actually want discipline. Regardless of how strong-willed they appear to be at times, even teenagers desire discipline. It is surprising to discover how many parents have failed to realize the true foundation for discipline. Many believe that constantly punishing a child will foster discipline. Though it is essential that parents punish disobedient children, it is important to realize that punishment is only a temporary solution. **In the long run, true discipline will only manifest itself when a child not** only realizes that certain actions are wrong, but also understands why they are wrong. For example, children need to be taught more than bully behavior itself is unacceptable. Children need to understand and actually consider how this behavior would affect them if the tables were turned, and they found themselves to be the victims. The bottom line is that it is vital that you help your child understand that he/she must be sensitive to how his/her actions affect others. A child who is taught and exercises such discernment is, by far, less likely to bully others.

SCHOOL'S RESPONSIBILITY

You may recall that nearly 160,000 students purposely skip school daily in the United States. In addition, approximately 20% of the children in school often avoid various campus areas. These children do not necessarily have a fear of being involved in school shootings or bombings, but they do fear persecution and harassment from other students. It is no secret that the majority of our schools are understaffed, and teachers are underpaid. However, regardless of these obstacles, educators must work diligently in their efforts to provide students with the safe and positive learning environment that they deserve.

Obviously all schools should have a system involving the implementation of policies that assure a safe physical environment (i.e., zero tolerance for weapons or fighting.)

Additionally, schools must take a proactive approach, to provide each student with, what is considered, a "SAFE CLIMATE." **What is equally important as a physically safe environment is a psychologically safe environment**. In other words, enforcing student handbooks or set rules may assist in creating a safe school, but they fall short if each student does not "feel" safe. The following are four specific areas that all educators should address that will assist in providing safe climates for our children at school.

- Surveying -

An effective place for a school to start a bully prevention program is with school wide surveys. Anonymous student surveys can serve as very effective tools for assessing the overall climate of a school. By coordinating a small task force consisting of students, parents, teachers, and if available subject experts, this collaborative group can create a survey compiled of various questions concerning bullying, as well as other school safety issues. For example, students could be asked if they have been bullied, witnessed bullying, or even bullied someone themselves. The survey could also inquire how often the student has been bullied, where most of the bullying took place, and if he informed anyone, as well as what was done. The list can go on and on. Though not all students will answer surveys truthfully, most students tend to answer questions more honestly if they are not required to reveal their own identity. **Though creating, distributing, and assessing school-wide surveys can be difficult, as well as time consuming, the information** they provide can prove to be invaluable to a school, as they create strategies to combat difficult issues, such as school bullying.

-Open Communication -

Just as important as family communication, school administrators and faculty must make an effort to establish open communication between themselves and the students they oversee. **First of all, school faculties must communicate clearly to all students what they define as bullying, and that no form of this behavior will be tolerated in their school.** Also, students should be informed of the repercussions involved if such incidents arise. Secondly, faculties must develop a trustful and caring relationship with students, which can assure students that teachers are willing to listen to them when they are faced with certain problems (such as bullying), and that they are concerned with assisting the student in solving these problems. Such relationships also encourage students to inform the faculty of various school issues or situations, rather than just "looking the other way." For example, even though a particular student may not be involved, he may witness others being bullied. Students should be encouraged that informing a faculty of such situations is brave and honorable rather than shameful "snitching." **The bottom line is that teachers and administrations that are willing to be attentive to the needs and concerns of its students, and also conveys to these students what is expected of them as a "responsible student" will most often create the safe school climate that all children truly deserve.**

- Level Playing Fields -

It is obvious that children must learn respect, respect for themselves, their teachers, as well as other students. To create a level playing field, educators must do more than inform students that they should respect others. Educators must implement programs into their core curriculum that will stress the importance of respect for other people, their things, as well as their feelings. Also, it should reinforce these essential principles. Teachers themselves have a responsibility to create and maintain a level playing field for students. **Teachers must avoid exercising partiality to individuals or groups based on various attributes (i.e., school athletes, academic achievers, etc. . . .) Obviously, there will always be certain children who appear to be brighter and possess a more positive attitude toward school**. Such children have a tendency to formulate better relationships with teachers. **While it is healthy for teachers to encourage such children, they should not do so to the extent that they alienate those who may not be so well adjusted at school.** The point is that schools consist of many different students with many different backgrounds. While these students will achieve many different levels of personal success later in life, during their developmental school years, they must feel that they are all on equal ground.

- **Protocol** -

Before considering protocol, it is important to note that stiff punishment alone, while necessary, is not the most effective means for deterring bullying. While it can be quite effective in the short run, the most effective long-term remedy is prevention. Educating students about the harmful effects of bullying, and teaching students to respect others, should be a school administration's focus toward prevention. While prevention is obviously the goal, it is unrealistic for those within the school system to believe that they can eliminate "all" forms of bulling. Also, to wait for the incidents to occur and then attempt to handle them is equally unrealistic. Keeping in mind that not every bullying situation will be the same, most will share very common characteristics. For this reason, it is essential that all schools have designated protocol for handling bully situations. **This protocol should include predetermined steps for teachers to follow when they discover bully situations themselves or are informed by students that bullying is occurring**. **This protocol should also include an appropriate punishment plan for those children who choose to bully others.** A school system that has a set plan for handling bullying can most often recognize potential problems at their onset and diffuse them before they escalate into more serious or uncontrollable situations.

The following is an example of a five-step plan for addressing bullying incidents in school.

EXAMPLE OF BULLYING PROTOCOL

Step One: **Communicate**

Gather and assess information to confirm actual bullying versus merely confrontational arguments

Step Two: **Mediate**

Bring together all of those involved in an attempt to diffuse the situation

Step Three: Separate

Restrict any interaction between the children involved, until situation is resolved

Step Four: **Negotiate**

If necessary, involve children's parents to discuss possible solutions as well as potential punishment

Step Five: **Terminate**

Final step leading to punishment based on severity of incident   (i.e., temporary or permanent suspension)

CHILD'S RESPONSIBILITY

Because there are obviously many more pupils than teachers or administrators, students have a tremendous responsibility concerning school bullying. Recall that, punishment for school infractions, such as bullying, is only a temporary solution. **To have a lasting effect on bully prevention, children must learn to be "responsible students."** Bullying, like so many other social issues, cannot be "policed" away. Instead, attitudes must not merely be adjusted, but changed all together. The following are five specific areas that are essential for changing attitudes of children toward themselves, others, as well as the subject of bullying. It is important that children not only know that these principles must be understood, but that they also must be exercised.

-Respect-

No matter how much children are taught or even punished, when they are outside of adult supervision, they are ultimately in a position in which they can and most often do make their own decisions. With this freedom comes responsibility and that responsibility is to demonstrate respect toward others. This includes respecting others' things, another person, and their feelings. **The bottom line is that everyone should learn to treat others the way they themselves would like to be treated.**

-Accountability-

Even younger children need to learn that they should be held accountable for their actions. You may recall one factor, which motivates some bullies, is simply anger. **The child who learns that he/she must be accountable for his/her actions, as a result of anger, is more likely to control that anger without lashing out at other people.** Children must learn that the key to effective conflict resolution is anger management. When they fail to exercise such self-control, they must understand the repercussions.

-Code of Silence-

You can probably recall that back in your own school days that it usually did not require much more than someone yelling the word "fight" in order to draw a big crowd. Bullying incidents are similar in that most children who bully are doing so in an attempt to prove something to those around them. In fact, in order for most bullying to continue, there must be an audience. The problem is that most, if not all in the audience, are unwilling to inform teachers as to what has occurred. **Whether due to fear of being bullied themselves or simply a lack of concern for the victim, most children choose to exercise the sacred "code of silence," whereby students do not tell on other students.** When other students realize how wrong bullying is, refuse to be an audience to such actions, and in turn break the code of silence by reporting those incidents to their teachers, a large percentage of bullying situations will subside.

- Anger Management -

The present hurtles that we face when considering child anger is basically twofold. On one extreme, you may have a child who allows anger to completely control him/her, often causing him/her to demonstrate improper outward behavior (i.e., violently lashing out at others). On the other extreme, you may find that a child gets angry very easily and chooses to suppress or internalize that anger. While both of these extremes are unhealthy, it is surprising to many to discover that children who suppress their anger may potentially pose the greatest threat. When this particular child allows anger to build, he/she is often building up more and more aggression. This child, when he/she reaches a point where he/she releases that aggression, has a tendency to be much more physically violent toward others. **The strategy that children must learn concerning anger management is that there is nothing necessarily wrong with anger**. It is an emotion that is as essential as trust, love, or fear. However, children must understand that aside from "physically" defending themselves, it is never appropriate nor acceptable to physically attack someone for any reason, much less out of anger. The bottom line is that children must learn to understand, accept, and communicate their anger, thus learning to control it rather than allow it to control them.

- Conflict Resolution -

Many bullying incidents are simply a result of conflicts between children. Though there can be many factors, oftentimes children do not know how to settle such conflicts between themselves. This leads to anger and frustration, thus often leading to physical violence. **First of all, it is vital that children of all ages learn and understand that violence is never the answer for resolving personal conflicts.** Secondly, while it is important that children learn how to deal with difficult situations, it is not only acceptable, but often necessary that they involve a trusted adult, someone who can serve as a mediator in order to assist in diffusing the conflict.

CHAPTER FIVE

School Bullying Check List

CHILD'S RESPONSIBILITY

- ☐ Understand and demonstrate respect toward others
- ☐ Be accountable for your own actions
- ☐ Break the "code of silence" by informing faculty of bullying incidents
- ☐ Exercise Anger Management by talking about your problems rather than lashing out
- ☐ Understand that physical violence does more to complicate a problem rather than resolve it

SCHOOL'S RESPONSIBILITY

- ☐ Conduct initial and ongoing school-wide surveys to assess a school's climate
- ☐ Create and maintain open communication between students and faculty
- ☐ Maintain level playing fields among all students
- ☐ Establish predetermined protocol for handling situations, as well as punishment plans

PARENT'S RESPONSIBILITY

- ☐ Lead your children by example
- ☐ Promote your child's self-esteem by looking for and encouraging his/her strong points
- ☐ Exercise open communication and always be prepared and available to listen
- ☐ Exercise Discipline

Chapter Six

The
Unthinkable

6

CHAPTER SIX

The Unthinkable

Obviously the tone of this book has been focused on prevention. While no one likes to think of his/her child as a victim, this program would not be complete without including measures that can and should be taken in the event that your child is victimized. Though we work diligently to prevent such incidents, we should realize that many occurrences will continue. **While the steps found in this chapter are not necessarily all inclusive, they do provide an effective foundation for which to build, in the event that the unthinkable does happen to your child.**

- **Sexual Abuse**
- **Child Abduction**
- **Internet Victimization**
- **School Bullying**

SEXUAL ABUSE

Considering that children can sometimes misinterpret certain situations, the first step concerning sexual abuse, especially when reporting incidents, is to thoroughly assess the situation to determine if in fact the abuse has occurred. I would like to note that, even if you do not have sufficient evidence to report incidents to the authorities, it is essential that you take the appropriate measures yourself. **In other words, if your child informs you that someone has touched him/her or made him/her feel uncomfortable, you should separate your child from that person, even though you may not have evidence that would substantiate criminal charges.** The following are three essential steps that should be taken if you discover that your child has been sexually abused.

- Provide Emotional Support -

First and foremost you must assure your child that what has occurred is by no means his/her fault and that he/she has done a courageous thing by telling you about the abuse. Child predators are notorious for implanting guilt into their victims. For this reason, many victims of sexual abuse live the rest of their lives lacking trust and feeling guilty for something that they truly had no control. While professional and psychological help may be required in some cases, one should never dismiss the importance and effectiveness of a loving and nurturing family that can assist a child in recovering from this heinous type of child abuse. The bottom line is that children are very resilient and can, with the proper emotional support, recover from acts of sexual abuse.

- Contact Authority -

You may recall that there are a number of reasons why an adult may fail to report the sexual abuse of a child. However, it is essential that you realize that anyone guilty of sexually abusing a child MUST be brought to justice. No only so he will face the penalty for what he has done, but also to prevent that individual from victimizing another child. It is worth repeating that the child predator lives a predatory lifestyle, and if not stopped, he will victimize other children. **Regardless of the damage that can be done to a person's name, reputation, or career, any person who victimizes a child should be reported to the authorities.**

- Seek Medical Attention -

Though in most cases, a child may not appear to be physically harmed by his/her abuser, medical attention may be required regardless. **Medical attention is not only for the purpose of treating a potential injury, but also for the gathering and documentation of evidence.**

CHILD ABDUCTION

No one wants to imagine that a child could ever be taken away without a trace. The thought of such an act brings paralyzing fear to any parent. What all parents need to realize is that time and lack of preparation are the primary obstacles concerning the safe recovery of an abducted child. The following are three vital steps that should be taken if such a horrific event occurs.

- Contact the Local Authorities -

The Federal Bureau of Investigations reports that approximately 75% of abducted children, that are murdered, are murdered within the initial three hours following the abduction. Therefore, the first step is to contact the local authorities IMMEDIATELY. **Contrary to what most people think, there is no waiting period required before a child can be reported missing and placed in the missing person's database.**

The information shared with local authorities should include a current photo of your child, as well as a detailed description of what he/she was last wearing. Additionally you should be specific concerning any possible identifying marks on your child, such as a scar or a birthmark. Recent video footage can also be very beneficial if you are able to involve the local media.

You should also inquire as to whether your local law enforcement agency is prepared to utilize and activate an

"AMBER ALERT." The Amber Alert is a cooperative program between law enforcement agencies and area broadcasters, whereby information concerning abduction cases, which meet specific criteria, are broadcasted through the local Emergency Alert System (EAS). The Emergency Alert System, which serves as a warning tool for severe weather, sends an urgent alert informing the broadcasting area of the abduction and shares descriptive information of the abductor and vehicle, etc.... Therefore, this allows an entire community to be on the look out for a missing child, in addition to law enforcement officers.

- Contact Outside Organization -

Immediately following the report to local authorities, you should consider contacting outside organizations as well. The most authoritative organization concerning child abductions is "The National Center for Missing and Exploited Children." While most law enforcement agencies have dealt with very few, if any, abduction cases, the NCMEC handles literally thousands of them every year. The information, support, and free services offered by the center are invaluable. **The number for contacting the National Center for Missing and Exploited Children is 1-800-THE-LOST (843-5678).**

- Surround Yourself with Family and Friends -

During such a traumatizing event, one should note the necessity of family and friends. They obviously will offer emotional support during a time when everything seems to suddenly fall apart. Additionally, family and friends can also assist by being in charge of follow ups on various information given to the authorities, as well as assuring contacts have been made to involve local media.

INTERNET VICTIMIZATION

The Internet is now quickly becoming one of the child predators most effective tools. Recall that the NCMEC states that approximately one out of every four children, using the Internet, receives some type of unsolicited sexually explicit material. Receiving this type of objectionable material can be quite disturbing to children and parents alike. **Though not being able to actually see who is sending this type of material, often leaves one feeling vulnerable and literally helpless; rest assured you are not.** The following are three specific guidelines that you should follow if you are faced with illegal material, such as child pornography or pedophilia-type material.

- Always Avoid Responding -

The first step for handling illegal Internet victimization is not necessarily something you should do, but rather something you must not do. Most often a child predator will distribute material randomly, as a form of "bait." Responding to the material, even with a negative response, is literally taking the bait, consequently offering the sender a direct link to you. **Therefore, NEVER show your disapproval for objectionable material by attempting to contact the sender.**

- Contact Authority -

The Department of Justice, as well as various branches of governmental agencies and organizations, are constantly monitoring the Internet for child pornography and pedophilia rings. In the event that your child is solicited by an adult to engage in child pornography or any form of sexual acts, you can and should contact these organizations to report the incident. You will be required to give information concerning the solicitation. It may also be necessary to provide personal information so that someone investigating the incident can contact you, in order to learn specifics pertaining to the illegal solicitation.

Also, keep in mind that in order to avoid abusing such services and reducing its effectiveness, as well as efficiency, it should not be used to report merely objectionable material. The organizations are designed to investigate specific illegal material, such as obvious child pornography and pedophilia-type material and solicitations. **The Web site for reporting "illegal" victimization against children on the Internet is www.cybertipline.com**

-Offer Emotional Support-

It is important to note that, while improper Internet solicitations may not physically harm a child, they can and usually are quite damaging nonetheless. If your child is exposed to illegal or even legal objectionable material, it is essential that you offer him/her support and comfort. Sadly enough, this comfort may include the necessity of explaining some subjects to which children are most often much too young to be exposed. For most, this comfort will simply be the reassurance you can offer them, that as a parent, you are there to support and protect them. Also, it is important that your child understands that it is not his/her fault that he/she received the objectionable material.

SCHOOL BULLYING

The key to resolving a bully situation is to recognize and respond to the incident at its onset, rather than allow it to escalate. However, before any steps can be taken to resolve school bullying, it is necessary to thoroughly assess the entire situation. You must first distinguish the difference between basic child arguments and disagreements versus actual bullying. Once persistent bullying is confirmed, it is essential that, as a parent, you approach the incident logically. Rather than outwardly demonstrating your own anger, you must respond as calmly and rationally as possible. **Obviously, it is very disturbing to discover that your child is the victim of a school bully, and it is quite difficult to hide your frustration.** However, you must not lose sight of the fact that your primary responsibility is to diffuse this situation rather than escalate it, by projecting your own anger toward your child, your child's school, or even the child that is the bully. Also, you should realize that there are no set patterns for resolving every bully situation. Though there may be extreme cases where the only option is to remove your child from the situation (i.e., change classes or transfer to another school), such a drastic measure is seldom the most practical or necessary solution.

Similar to previous steps offered in this chapter, the following are not necessarily all inclusive. However, based on the result of various incident studies, as well as their outcome, the following steps offer effective means for resolving bullying between children in school.

- Contact Child's Teacher -

You may notice that the first step to resolving school bullying is to contact your child's teacher rather than the other child's parents. The present hurtles often faced when contacting parents is that more often than not, parents will defend their own child, whether they are right or wrong. On the other hand, your child's teacher should be capable of approaching the incident with an impartial attitude. **The purpose of contacting the teacher is not merely to bring the seriousness of the incident to his/her attention, but to also encourage that teacher to speak to the students separately, as well as together, in order to assist in resolving the conflict.** The goal is to settle the conflict as soon as it is recognized. It is during this early stage that most situations can be resolved most efficiently. Also, as a courtesy to your child's teacher, it is appropriate that when a situation is resolved, you contact that teacher to inform him/her of the success of the mediation.

- Contact School Administration -

What could be considered the second step to resolving conflict is to contact your child's school administrators (i.e., school principal or counselor). It is important to note that the purpose of contacting school administration is not to report a teacher who appears unconcerned with this issue. **Oftentimes, bullying situations, left unchecked, escalate to a degree that a teacher speaking with the students brings little resolution.** Such cases may lead to the necessity of organizing a conference between the children involved, as well as the parents, consequently requiring school administrators to serve as mediator. The purpose of these conferences is to inform the parents about the seriousness of child bullying, as well as the school's policy for punishing students if the problem continues.

- Encourage Your Child -

Bullying situations can and sometimes are quite traumatizing to a child. Putting a stop to a bullying incident may not be enough. As a parent, you also have a responsibility to assure your child recovers. After being the victim of persistent bullying, sometimes a child develops an extremely low self-image. This child may believe that there is something wrong with him/her, and that he/she actually invited the bullying. Furthermore, with situations involving extreme mental and verbal abuse, a child may begin to believe all the negative things the bully said about him/her. If this attitude is left unchecked, it can have a lifelong negative effect on a child. The key to overcoming these ill effects is to offer your child unconditional support and encouragement. **Believe it or not, a child can, with the proper parental involvement, come away from a bullying incident even more confident, by simple realizing what he/she has overcome.**

CHAPTER SIX

The Unthinkable Check List

SEXUAL ABUSE

☐ Provide your child with emotional support

☐ Separate your child from abuser and contact authority

☐ If necessary, seek medical attention

CHILD ABDUCTION

☐ Contact local authorities immediately

☐ Contact outside organization (NCMEC)

☐ Surround yourself with family and friends

INTERNET VICTIMIZATION

☐ Never respond to illegal or objectionable material

☐ Contact Authority (www.cybertipline.com)

☐ Comfort and reassure your child concerning the incident, as well as the information, to which he/she may have been exposed

SCHOOL BULLYING

☐ Contact your child's teacher

☐ Contact school administration

☐ Encourage your child to ensure he/she recovers from the incident

Chapter Seven

Teaching

Effectively

7

CHAPTER SEVEN

Teaching Effectively

I t deserves repeating that when dealing with child safety; the actual child should share the least amount of the responsibility. However, while children should be allowed to enjoy a carefree life, they do need to take "some" responsibility for their own safety. **One must keep in mind that no matter how much you attempt to protect or shelter your child, if a situation arises without you being there, that child must be prepared to protect him/herself.** This section includes five basic principles, which will assist you in effectively educating your child about the various areas of personal safety. Recall that an educated child leads to a confident child, which in turn leads to a safe child.

- **Avoid Scare Tactics**
- **Teachable Moments**
- **Age-Specific Instruction**
- **Continual Reinforcement**
- **Scenario-Based Training**

AVOID SCARE TACTICS

The key to effectively teaching children specific safety principles is to present the information in a non-threatening format. Threatening teaching methods, often referred to as "scar tactics," may appear to have an initial effect. However, such methods offer no long-term benefits. For example, a parent may want his/her child to stay away from strangers. This parent may inform the child that strangers want to take him/her away from the family, so he/she will never see them again. This method may scare a child to a level that he/she will make sure that he/she will avoid strangers. Initially this seems effective, but before long, the child's fear will usually fade, as well as the caution that accompanied that fear. There are also children who have a tendency to be at the other extreme. These children may be faced with the same scare tactic and become so overwhelmed with paranoia that they have difficulties functioning in various social environments. An example could be a child who has become so frightened by scare tactics that he/she will never want to leave his/her home. **The point is that child safety is obviously a very serious subject and discussing such issues can be potentially disturbing to both parent and child. However, it is essential that you do not force your fears on your child, by attempting to use scare tactics.**

TEACHABLE MOMENTS

Obviously there are times when it is necessary for adults to "lay down the law" with children. For their own safety, oftentimes, we must simply present set rules and guidelines, which children must follow. Though such instruction is essential, it is important to understand that children of all ages appear to be much more receptive to instruction at different moments in time. **There are times when children seem to be inquisitive about certain subjects**. When a child's curiosity or interest is "sparked" about a specific subject or issue, the instruction he/she receives, at that particular time, often has a lasting effect. The key to long lasting personal instruction is to look for "teachable moments."

AGE SPECIFIC

I am often asked, "At what age should a child begin learning personal safety?" In addition, many parents want to know exactly how to teach the younger versus the older children. **It should be obvious that various age-groups require different methods of instruction.** While children in the preschool through third grade age-group may respond better to short-term verbal instruction, as well as visual aids (i.e., flash cards, activity books), older children may consider such methods trivial or immature. These older children may require more mental stimulation and respond more positively to detailed verbal instruction, which includes interactive communication (i.e., question and answer sessions). **Regardless of the methods of instruction, the primary difference between teaching various age-groups is the explicit details required in the instruction**. Though it may be acceptable to talk to young teens or even some preteens about the specifics of sexual abuse, or exactly what a child abductor may do, this should not be the case for younger children. Discussing details that are too explicit can force a young child to consider situations or subjects about which he/she may have never thought. Such instruction can only add to additional fears for the child. The bottom line is that once you design your instruction to not only be tactful, but also age-specific, a child is never too young to learn child safety.

CONTINUAL REINFORCEMENT

I can testify from years of experience and literally thousands of teaching sessions that the so called "one-hit" instruction strategies are not very effective methods for teaching children. It doesn't require many years of teaching or parenting to witness first hand just how quickly a child forgets the instructions given to him/her. Of course, oftentimes, even young children exercise a "selective" memory and purposely "forget" specific instructions, children quite often fail to absorb information given to them, and unless given to them regularly, they simply forget it.

Regardless of how well a child can recite rules back to you or even apply specific principles at that particular time, without reinforcement, there will seldom be any long-term benefit.

SCENARIO-BASED TRAINING

Scenario-based training (situation assessment) is not only an effective method of teaching, but it is also a very effective way of assuring that a child understands specific safety principles. **Scenario training is a technique, whereby you encourage children to consider specific safety situations, and then you allow them to explain what they would do if they were found in that situation.** Notice that I stated not what they "should" do, but what they "would" do. Such methods of training not only demonstrate what areas you may need to work on with your children, but also through their feedback, you can better understand some of their specific fears or concerns. In addition, children are given the opportunity, through roll playing, to recognize various situations in advance, and in turn respond to these situations. In order for situation assessment to be effective, the situations must be realistic. However, you should always keep in mind how old the child you are teaching is and keep details age-specific. **The bottom line is, rather than force children to be on the receiving end of large amounts of information, allow them to interact** with your instructions. Using scenario-based training, through involvement, will keep a child's interest in the overall teaching process, which will assist in him/her in absorbing the material, as well as applying it.

CHAPTER SEVEN

Teaching Effectively Check List

- ☐ Be tactful with instruction

- ☐ Keep material age-specific

- ☐ Do not force fears on your child

- ☐ Look for "Teachable moments"

- ☐ Listen to your child

- ☐ Utilize scenario-based training

Conclusion

As unsettling as it is to accept, there is no set equation that will guarantee that our children will be 100 percent safe. No one has all of the answers. Nonetheless, it is our responsibility to do all we can, in order to protect those who cannot protect themselves. **Regardless of which area of safety we are discussing, the task of protecting our children is great**. However, I believe that our strong will and determination can be greater. It is my hope that by coordinating the principles contained in this book with responsible parenting and teaching, we can be confident that we are doing all we can in order to protect our most precious gifts, our children.

"Our Children Our Responsibility"
Timothy C. Derby
2311 Highway 45 North, Suite D
Columbus, MS 39705
662-327-5425
www.safecarechildren.com

INDEX

A

Q

R